PRACTICE *Vocabulary*

Milada Broukal

THOMSON
™
HEINLE

Australia Canada Mexico Singapore Spain United Kingdom United States

THOMSON

HEINLE

PRACTICE *Vocabulary*
Milada Broukal

Vice President, Editorial Director ESL:
Nancy Leonhardt

Director of School Publishing:
Edward Lamprich

Managing Developmental Editor:
Donna Schaffer

Developmental Editors:
Tania Maundrell-Brown
Michele McGrath

Contributing Editor:
Jill Ortman

Marketing Manager:
John Ade

Production Editor:
Jeff Freeland

Manufacturing Coordinator:
Kerry Burke

Designer/Compositor:
Roberta Landi Book Production

Illustrator:
Len Shalansky

Cover Designer:
Ha Nguyen

Printer:
Mazer

Cover Art: Meditation on Squares #111 by Kurt Glowienke. Used with permission of the artist.

Photo Credits:

Photos on pages 21 & 89 are Digital Imagery © copyright 2001 Photodisc, Inc.

Corbis Images photos: page 39 © Bettmann/CORBIS, page 55 © Bettmann/CORBIS, page 77 © Bettmann/CORBIS, page 101 © Hulton-Deutsch Collection/CORBIS

Contents

To the Teacher

PRACTICE *Vocabulary* is designed to be used by students who have reached an intermediate level of competency in English grammar. The text is for both self-study and classroom use.

Vocabulary-building skills are presented in a theme-based context, which allows students to increase their vocabulary while acquiring knowledge about a variety of subjects. Reading passages not only provide a context for the skills that are presented, but also serve to familiarize students with the vocabulary and style of academic content areas. High-interest exercises are included with each chapter to build up student confidence in usage and to allow you to assess student proficiency.

Chapters 1 through 4 introduce students to the basic skills needed for deciphering unfamiliar items. By learning to use context, roots, and affixes to figure out new words, students will become less dependent on their dictionaries. The direction lines will alert students when they should consult their dictionaries to complete certain exercises. Many of the words in PRACTICE *Vocabulary* can be found in the *Newbury House Dictionary*. Some words, however, will not be found in a learner's dictionary, but can be found in a more complete, or unabridged, dictionary.

Chapters 5 through 10 are theme-based. These chapters not only provide students with specific vocabulary, but also teach them to group words with similar meanings.

The final chapter deals with idioms, confusing expressions, and word pairs. These have been placed later in the book because of the difficulty they may present for some less experienced speakers. However, you may introduce them earlier if you feel your students can benefit from your doing so.

A separate Answer Key for both the chapter exercises and the end-of-chapter tests is available.

Chapter Structure

Reading passage

The reading passages present information that is interesting and appropriate for students. They provide the context upon which the vocabulary is based.

Strategies for vocabulary development

Strategies are presented that deal with the particular vocabulary-building focus of the chapter.

Exercises

There are a variety of exercise types: multiple choice, fill-in-the-blank, correcting errors, completing word lists, true or false questions, and dictionary work. These exercises can be done in the classroom with students interacting in pairs or groups, or they can be assigned as homework.

End of Chapter Tests

The end-of-chapter tests focus on the vocabulary taught in the chapter. They will help you evaluate student success in acquiring new material.

How to Use This Book

1. Order of presentation

The units in this book do not have to be covered in the order presented. You can either follow the order of the book or choose the units that tie in with your curriculum.

2. Classroom use

The introductory passages and/or dialogues, with the questions and tasks that follow, can be used for interactive work with students in groups or pairs. If listening skills need to be worked on, you can read the passages and the dialogues aloud. After going over the strategies with the students, the exercises can be either worked on in the classroom or assigned as homework.

3. Use of dictionaries

The use of a good dictionary is encouraged and students are alerted to use one by the exercise direction line. We do, however, recommend that students use dictionaries only after they have tried to work out the meaning of a word by themselves, through context or other clues.

4. Student vocabulary notebooks

Students should be encouraged to keep a personal vocabulary notebook. They should build their own vocabulary lists based on the words that are most useful for them.

To the Student

You can use PRACTICE *Vocabulary* for both self-study and in a classroom with a teacher. This book gives clear and simple explanations, examples, and exercises that will help you learn vocabulary-building skills and how to interpret unfamiliar words. Watch for the *Strategy* boxes. They have summaries and suggestions that will help you learn and retain new words. Each chapter has exercises and an end-of-chapter test so you can practice using what you've learned. Sometimes, you will be asked to consult a dictionary to complete an exercise. You will find many of the words in PRACTICE *Vocabulary* in the *Newbury House Dictionary*. Some words, however, will not be found in a learner's dictionary, but can be found in a more complete, or unabridged, dictionary.

Strategies for Vocabulary Building

Read as much as you can

By reading as many magazines, books (both fiction and nonfiction), and journals as you can, you will encounter new words. You can guess the meanings of many of these words by their context—that is, you can get a clue to the meaning from the words that surround the new word. If you remain unsure of a word's meaning, you can look up the word in your dictionary to check if you were right.

Use a good English dictionary

It is better not to use a bilingual one. A good dictionary should include the following information about a word:

 a) its pronunciation
 b) its part of speech (noun, adjective, verb, etc.)
 c) a clear, simple definition
 d) an example of the word in a sentence or phrase

More advanced speakers will also want their dictionary to include word origins.

Learn roots, prefixes, and suffixes

Roots and prefixes from Latin and Greek make up many English words. Prefixes are added to the beginning of a root and suffixes are added to the end to modify the meanings of words. Learning these will help you increase your vocabulary.

Learn from listening

Listening to good programs on the radio and television, as well as to people who speak English well, is another way of improving your vocabulary. Since you can't always ask the speaker to tell you what a particular word means, write down any words you don't know and look them up later.

Use a dictionary of synonyms and antonyms (a thesaurus)

Synonyms are words that have almost the same meaning; antonyms are words that have almost the opposite meaning. If you are using a computer, try using the "Thesaurus" tool. You will find lists of synonyms, and sometimes antonyms, here. Knowing a word's synonyms and antonyms will expand your vocabulary. Some dictionaries of synonyms and antonyms explain each word and how it differs in meaning from its synonyms. Since no two words have the exact same meaning, this can be very useful .

Make your own word list

Get a notebook for your vocabulary study and use it to create your own word list. Whenever you come across a word you don't know, write it down in your notebook, along with the sentence in which you found it. Try to work out the meaning of the word from its context. Then look the word up in a dictionary and write the definition in your notebook. Also write down any other information, such as the root of the word, and see how it is connected to the meaning. Last, write your own sentence using the word. Writing will help you remember the word and its meaning. Try to add a new word to your list every day.

Create your own theme groups

Words are easier to remember and learn when you group them with other words that have similar meanings. For example,

Words describing feeling good about something:

be fond of

devoted to

cherish

adore

Then you can make another theme with the opposite.

Words describing feeling bad about something:

detest

loathe

abhor

repel

despise

disgust

Use your new words

Using your new words, whether in speaking or writing, is an important step in learning them.

Chapter 1
Words in Context

When you don't know the meaning of a word and there is no prefix, suffix, or root to help you figure it out, look at the word's *context*.

The context of the word is its setting. It is where we *hear* it in speech or *see* it in writing. Hearing or seeing words in context is one of the ways we learn words. Learning to figure out the meaning of words will help you increase your vocabulary.

The following reading passages include exercises for learning words in context. Try to figure out the words using the strategies suggested below, in addition to your dictionary.

Strategies

- When you're looking for clues to the meaning of a word in context, one of these types of *contextual* clues will help you:

  Straight definitions
  Sometimes when an unusual word is used in a text, a definition of the word appears close by. Try to understand the definition and apply it to the word in context.

  Paraphrase or synonyms
  Look for the possibility of another word or phrase in the context that has the same meaning.

  Implied meaning
  Sometimes direct clues are not given in the text, but are hinted at or *implied*. In this case, think about the context and guess what the meaning of the word might be. Even if you aren't sure of the exact meaning, you should be able to get a general idea of what it means.

- Every time you read, practice looking for contextual clues. This will help you learn to think about the meaning of what you read, and will also train you to think about words and their meanings.

Reading About Science

Dirty Snowballs

Astronomers sometimes call comets "dirty snowballs" because they are made of ice and dust. The comet's tail is made up of dust **particles.** The ice melts as the comet comes close to the sun and these particles are released. The tails of some comets stretch out for millions of kilometers into space. Other comets have tails that are so short they are almost **invisible.**

Sometimes we see light **streak** across the sky. This is called a "falling star." We are actually seeing meteors. They are small solid objects that look like balls of fire. Meteors appear in a range of colors, including yellow, orange, red, and even green. The color is **determined** by the speed of the meteor, not by its **composition.**

Meteoroids are the smallest particles orbiting the sun. They are no bigger than a **grain** of sand. Meteoroids become visible when they reach the Earth's atmosphere and become meteors. **Friction,** caused by air particles hitting the fast-moving meteoroids, makes them **glow** blue or white. They are **rarely** seen for more than a few seconds, as they usually burn up before they reach the Earth's atmosphere.

Exercise 1

Find the words below in the passage above. Try to figure out the meaning of the words using contextual clues. Then circle the letter of the correct definition.

1. particles

    (a) pieces of space

    (b) pieces of matter

2. invisible

    (a) not able to be seen

    (b) not able to be touched

3. streak

    (a) move slowly

    (b) move quickly

4. astronomers

    (a) scientists who study outer space

    (b) eye doctors

5. determined

    (a) chose

    (b) decided by

6. composition

    (a) its appearance

    (b) what it's made of

7. grain

    (a) a tiny piece

    (b) cereal

8. friction

    (a) mix slowly

    (b) rubbing

9. rarely

    (a) hardly ever

    (b) never

10. glow

    (a) give off light

    (b) emit sound

■■■ PRACTICE *Vocabulary*

Exercise 2

The following words have to do with small pieces or amounts. Write the correct word on the blank line. Some words will be used more than once. Use your dictionary if you need to.

grain	splinter	trace	blade
speck	flake	breath	item

1. _____ of sand

2. _____ of grass

3. _____ of dust

4. _____ of fresh air

5. _____ of snow

6. _____ of news

7. _____ of wood

8. _____ of poison

9. _____ of perfume

10. _____ of salt

Exercise 3

Put the following words in order of size from the smallest (1) to the largest (5), according to the objects they describe.

Earth	meteor	solar system	galaxy	universe

1. _____

2. _____

3. _____

4. _____

5. _____

Reading About People

Jules Verne (1828–1905)

Jules Verne is often called "the father of science fiction." He was born in 1828, in Nantes, France. While he was studying law in Paris, he discovered that he loved the theater. He decided to be a writer instead of a lawyer. He first had a play published in 1850.

Verne spent many hours studying engineering, *geology,* and astronomy. He used what he learned to make his *fiction* more *realistic.* His first *novel, Five Weeks in a Balloon*, was very successful. The novel *appealed* to nineteenth-century readers, who were extremely interested in science. Verne also wrote *Journey to the Center of the Earth, From the Earth to the Moon,* and *20,000 Leagues Under the Sea.*

Jules Verne did more than write *entertaining* stories. He also had a great *ability* to *anticipate* future inventions, such as submarines, trips into outer space, helicopters, and guided missiles. Verne said that his *object* was to write books that young people would *profit* from reading. He certainly achieved this goal.

Exercise 4

Find the words below in the passage above. Try to figure out the meaning of the words using contextual clues. Then circle the letter of the correct definition.

1. fiction
   - (a) true
   - (b) not true

2. appealed
   - (a) interested
   - (b) bothered

3. entertaining
   - (a) boring
   - (b) enjoyable

4. anticipate
   - (a) know in advance
   - (b) like

5. object
   - (a) purpose
   - (b) mistake

6. profit
   - (a) lose
   - (b) gain

7. geology
   - (a) study of music
   - (b) study of rocks

8. realistic
   - (a) false
   - (b) life-like

9. novel
   - (a) book-length story
   - (b) diary

10. ability
    - (a) power
    - (b) liking

PRACTICE *Vocabulary*

Exercise 5

Look up the following words in your dictionary and then complete each sentence with the correct word. Write the word on the blank line.

period	spell	terms	semester	era
century	span	decade	age	epoch

1. The _____ of space exploration started in the 1960s.

   (a) decade   **(b)** era   **(c)** spell

2. The computer _____ has helped improve global communication.

   (a) age   **(b)** terms   **(c)** span

3. The discovery of the Americas began _____ of adventure.

   (a) a semester   **(b)** a spell   **(c)** an epoch

4. From 1990 to the year 2000 was the last _____ of the twentieth century.

   (a) epoch   **(b)** decade   **(c)** span

5. Many colleges in the United States run on _____ system.

   (a) a decade   **(b)** an era   **(c)** a semester

6. The President of the United States can only serve two _____ of four years each.

   (a) epochs   **(b)** terms   **(c)** age

7. John Cabot was a great fifteenth-_____ explorer.

   (a) century   **(b)** age   **(c)** decade

8. The Civil War ended an important _____ of growth in American history.

   (a) period   **(b)** terms   **(c)** semester

9. The northern part of the country suffered from a terrible cold _____ in the winter of 1993.

   (a) terms   **(b)** spell   **(c)** era

10. The Pony Express lasted for a _____ of eighteen months.

   (a) terms   **(b)** spell   **(c)** span

Exercise 6

Circle the word in each group that does not belong.

1.	writer	author	poet	doctor
2.	geology	photography	astronomy	biology
3.	object	purpose	epoch	goal
4.	invent	create	desire	discover
5.	attractive	realistic	genuine	authentic

Reading About Social Studies

Apache Warriors

The Apaches were a Native American tribe that lived in New Mexico and Arizona. They were **nomads,** moving from place to place. They hunted buffalo, farmed, and **gathered** seeds. Food was often **scarce.**

The name "Apache" means "fighting men." The Apaches were great warriors. Boys began training for war when they were very young. They learned to **survive** in the **arid** desert, to stand guard for many hours, and to send smoke signals. Apache women taught their daughters to gather food, cook, and sew.

The Apaches fought to **maintain** their way of life. In 1848, New Mexico became part of the United States. The Apaches were unable to **defeat** the soldiers who were sent to fight against them. Finally, they were forced to live on **reservations.**

Many of the 50,000 Apaches who are alive today live on reservations in Arizona and New Mexico. Their **culture** is a mixture of traditional Apache and modern North American **customs.**

Exercise 7

Find the words below in the passage above. Try to figure out the meaning of the words using contextual clues. Then circle the letter of the correct definition.

1. nomad

   (a) a person who moves from place to place

   (b) a person who lives in one place

2. gathered

   (a) discarded

   (b) collected

■■■

3. scarce

   (a) limited

   (b) spoiled

4. survive

   (a) live

   (b) work

5. maintain

   (a) keep

   (b) lose

6. defeat

   (a) find

   (b) beat

7. reservation

   (a) a special area for Native Americans

   (b) a hotel

8. customs

   (a) taxes

   (b) special habits

9. arid

   (a) wet

   (b) dry

10. culture

   (a) ideas and behavior of a people or region

   (b) sports

Exercise 8

A *synonym* is a word that has the same (or almost the same) meaning as another word. An *antonym* has the opposite meaning. Use a dictionary of synonyms and antonyms, or a *thesaurus,* to help you complete the exercise.

List as many synonyms and antonyms as you can for the word ***scarce.***

SCARCE

Synonyms

insufficient

_____

_____

_____

_____

_____

_____

Antonyms

plentiful

_____

_____

_____

_____

_____

_____

Reading About History

Jamestown

Jamestown was the first **permanent** English colony in America. Captain John Smith and a group of English settlers **founded** it in 1607. They had a hard time in their new home. Many people died from **famine** and disease. Their neighbors, the Algonquin Indians, attacked them. The winter of 1609 was **particularly harsh.** It was called the "starving time" because food was so scarce. Only 60 of the **original** 214 colonists survived. The colony did not **prosper** until its most important **crop,** tobacco, was introduced.

The first representative meeting in America was held in Jamestown, Virginia, in 1619. The goal of the meeting was to start a government. The **village** grew and became the **capital** of Virginia. It remained an important settlement until the capital was moved to Williamsburg in 1698.

Exercise 9

Find the words below in the passage above. Try to figure out the meaning of the words using contextual clues. Then circle the letter of the correct definition.

1. permanent

   (a) temporary

   (b) lasting

2. founded

   (a) bought

   (b) started

3. famine

   (a) food shortage

   (b) feast

4. particularly

   (a) especially

   (b) a little

5. harsh

   (a) easy

   (b) severe

6. original

   (a) first

   (b) male

7. prosper

   (a) do well

   (b) starve

8. crop

   (a) meat

   (b) product

9. capital

   (a) main city

   (b) town

10. village

    (a) a small town

    (b) a large city

■■■

Exercise 10

Look up the following words in your dictionary and list them under the headings *Old* or *New*.

innovative modern	aged obsolete	antiquated original	novel mature	ancient fresh

Old   **New**

_____   _____

_____   _____

_____   _____

_____   _____

_____   _____

_____   _____

Exercise 11

Write an *antonym* on the blank line next to each of the following words.

1. permanent _____

2. founded _____

3. famine _____

4. original _____

5. prosper _____

Reading About Science

El Niño

El Niño appears every three to seven years. Peruvian fishermen first noticed it in the late 1800s. The Pacific Ocean became *unusually* warm and many fish died. Since it seemed to happen around Christmas, they named it after the "boy child," or Jesus.

At first the name El Niño was used for the warm *current* that *occurs* every December. Now it is only used to describe very *intense* and long-lasting *events.* Its full name is El Niño Southern Oscillation, or ENSO.

El Niño causes serious changes in the *climate.* The wet weather that is normal for the western Pacific moves to the east. The arid conditions that are normal for the east appear in the west. South America has heavy rainfall and parts of Asia, India, and Africa suffer from *droughts.*

Warm waters off the coast of Peru and Ecuador have very *negative* effects. The plants that the fish eat become scarce. This causes the fish to leave the area or to die. These fish are what the seabirds eat, so they leave, too. The fishermen of the area also lose their *source* of *income.* There are no fish to catch.

Exercise 12

Find the words below in the passage above. Try to figure out the meaning of the words using contextual clues. Then circle the letter of the correct definition.

1. unusually
   - (a) strangely
   - (b) normally

2. current
   - (a) root
   - (b) flow

3. occur
   - (a) happen
   - (b) become

4. intense
   - (a) weak
   - (b) strong

5. event
   - (a) happening
   - (b) sound

6. climate
   - (a) pattern
   - (b) weather

7. drought
   - (a) dryness
   - (b) moisture

8. negative
   - (a) good
   - (b) bad

9. income
   - (a) earnings
   - (b) family

10. source
    - (a) where something goes
    - (b) where something comes from

Exercise 13

Look up the following words in your dictionary and list them under the headings *Intense* or *Weak*.

fierce	concentrated	feeble	violent	powerless
flimsy	desperate	extreme	ineffectual	fragile

Intense   **Weak**

_____   _____

_____   _____

_____   _____

_____   _____

_____   _____

_____   _____

_____   _____

Exercise 14

Circle the letter of the correct word to complete each sentence.

1. During the drought, the trees died because there was not enough _____

    (a) moisture.   **(b)** snow.   **(c)** wind.   **(d)** dirt.

2. He lost his source of income, so he didn't have enough _____ to buy food.

    (a) time   **(b)** money   **(c)** effort   **(d)** interest

3. Air-conditioning is a kind of _____ control.

    (a) population   **(b)** animal   **(c)** climate   **(d)** water

4. It takes a lot of energy to swim against the _____

    (a) current.   **(b)** sand.   **(c)** plants.   **(d)** air.

5. Heavy rainfall can cause _____

    (a) income.   **(b)** droughts.   **(c)** climate.   **(d)** floods.

Reading About Science

Matter

Matter is anything that takes up *space* and has *mass.* Mass refers to how much there is of something. It has to do with *weight,* but is not the same thing. Everything around you is composed of matter. Your body is made up of matter. So are the foods you eat, and the air you breathe.

Matter has physical and chemical *properties.* Physical properties can be seen. If you look at a piece of wood, you can see its size, color, shape, and *density.* You cannot see its chemical properties. You would have to chemically change the wood to observe them.

Matter can be changed either physically or chemically. A physical change doesn't change the *type* of matter. When you *carve* a piece of wood, it changes its *appearance,* but it is still wood. A chemical change, however, turns one *substance* into another. When you burn a piece of wood, you cause chemical changes. You turn wood into *ash.* Chemical changes cannot be *reversed.* You can't turn ash back into a piece of wood.

Exercise 15

Find the words below in the passage above. Try to figure out the meaning of the words using contextual clues. Then circle the letter of the correct definition.

1. mass

    (a) quantity

    (b) huge

2. carve

    (a) sew

    (b) cut

3. weight

    (a) color

    (b) heaviness

4. property

    (a) characteristic

    (b) condition

5. density

    (a) transparency

    (b) mass per unit

6. appearance

    (a) how something looks

    (b) attendance

7. substance

    (a) kind of matter

    (b) standard

8. reverse

    (a) gear

    (b) change back

9. space

    (a) an empty area

    (b) a room

10. ash

    (a) the powder left after something burns

    (b) a piece of art

Exercise 16

A. All of these words mean *to see*, but they are used differently. Look up their definitions in your dictionary and then choose the correct word to complete each sentence. Write the word on the blank line.

observe   watch   witness   notice   look

1. As part of our experiment, we have to _____ the changes that take place as the seed develops into a plant.

2. If you _____ a crime, you should call the police.

3. Please _____ the time so that you are not late.

4. A vampire is afraid to _____ in a mirror.

5. You may _____ that the city has grown since the last time you were here.

B. *Homonyms* are words that sound alike and may be spelled alike, but have different meanings. Using your dictionary, find two different meanings for each of the following words. Write the definitions on the blank lines next to the words.

1. property _____

   _____

2. watch _____

   _____

3. matter _____

   _____

4. notice _____

   _____

5. present _____

   _____

Reading About Science

News Report: The Seattle Earthquake

At 10:54 in the morning, on February 28, 2001, a powerful earthquake hit Seattle, Washington. Buildings began to shake and *sway,* windows *rattled,* and floors *vibrated.* It lasted for forty seconds. It was the strongest earthquake in the *region* in fifty-two years.

    Seismologists said the quake measured 6.8 on the *Richter Scale.* The *epicenter* was near the city of Olympia. Luckily, the quake was deep beneath the ground. A shallow earthquake would have caused much more *damage.*

    School children knew what to do. They got under their desks and waited for the shaking to stop. Walls *collapsed,* windows *shattered,* rocks and plaster fell, but no one was killed. Most of the injured people had only cuts and bruises.

    It will cost more than $1 billion to repair all the damage caused by the earthquake. People agree that it could have been much worse. The earthquake that struck Los Angeles in 1994 killed 72 people and caused $25 billion in damage.

Exercise 17

Find the words below in the passage above. Try to figure out the meaning of the words using contextual clues. Then circle the letter of the correct definition.

1. sway

    (a) move back and forth

    (b) stand

2. rattle

    (a) open

    (b) make a noise

3. vibrate

    (a) stop

    (b) shake

4. seismologist

    (a) scientist who studies earthquakes

    (b) ear doctor

5. Richter Scale

    (a) a measurement of earthquakes

    (b) a scale for weighing rocks

6. epicenter

    (a) center of an earthquake

    (b) mall

7. region

    (a) lake

    (b) area

8. damage

    (a) result

    (b) harm

9. collapse

    (a) fall down

    (b) injure

10. shatter

    (a) break

    (b) spoil

Exercise 18

The following words mean *to damage* or *destroy*. Look them up in your dictionary and select the best two words to write under each heading. You may use the same word more than once.

hurt	impair	injure	spoil	ruin
harm	mar	damage	destroy	wreck

1. *A Chair*

   _____

   _____

2. *Your Leg*

   _____

   _____

3. *Your Reputation*

   _____

   _____

4. *The Environment*

   _____

   _____

5. *Your Health*

   _____

   _____

Exercise 19

The following words refer to different sounds. Circle the letter of the sound that is louder. Use your dictionary if you are not sure of the meaning of a word.

1. (a) hum
   (b) rumble

2. (a) roar
   (b) squeak

3. (a) rustle
   (b) rattle

4. (a) murmur
   (b) rumble

5. (a) bang
   (b) rustle

Reading About Literature

Poetry

There are many different kinds of poems. Poems may rhyme, but they don't have to. Poetry is divided into three types: *lyric, narrative,* and *dramatic.*

Lyric poetry is the most common kind. It includes most short poems. Lyrics may be set to music and sung. *Odes, elegies,* and *sonnets* are longer lyric poems. The ode is very structured. It may be written to **praise** a person or to **celebrate** an important event. Elegies have to do with death. Sonnets are fourteen-line poems with a special rhyme pattern. Often they are love poems.

Narrative poetry tells stories. The most important kinds of narrative poems are **ballads** and **epics.** Ballads tell stories about individuals. They are meant to be sung. The epic is probably the oldest form of poetry. Epics are long poems that tell about the **heroic deeds** of a character. "The Odyssey" is one of the best-known epics. Many cultures have epics about their histories and legends.

Dramatic poetry also tells stories, but the characters act out the **tales.** The **dialogue** is written in **rhyme.** Shakespeare is the most **famous** dramatic poet.

Exercise 20

Find the words below in the passage above. Try to figure out the meaning of the words using contextual clues. Then circle the letter of the correct definition.

1. praise

    (a) say nice things about

    (b) insult

2. ballad

    (a) a poem that is sung

    (b) a poem about death

3. epic

    (a) a short poem

    (b) a long poem

4. heroic

    (a) something brave

    (b) something from history

5. deed

    (a) story

    (b) achievement

6. tale

    (a) story

    (b) conversation

7. dialogue

    (a) conversation

    (b) thoughts

8. rhyme

    (a) a long poem

    (b) words that sound alike

9. celebrate

    (a) forget

    (b) honor

10. famous

    (a) well-known

    (b) serious

Exercise 21

Look up the following words in your dictionary and complete each sentence with the correct word. Write the word on the blank line.

verse	dialogue	prose	epic	rhyme
nursery rhyme	poet	lyric	monologue	meter

1. A long story full of brave deeds is a/an _____.

2. A person who writes poems is a/an _____.

3. A short story that is often sung is a/an _____ poem.

4. _____ is the rhythm of a poem.

5. Shakespeare's plays are written in _____.

6. Written language, not poetry, as in books and newspapers, is called

   _____.

7. A word or line that ends with the same sound as another is a/an

   _____.

8. A short well-known song or poem for young children is a/an

   _____.

9. A long speech or poem spoken by one person is a/an

   _____.

10. A written conversation in a book or play is a/an _____.

Exercise 22

Circle the word in each group that does not belong.

1. story   tale   anecdote   abridgement

2. fearless   heroic   accomplished   brave

3. personage   figure   dialogue   character

4. legend   fable   history   myth

5. dialogue   program   speech   monologue

End of Chapter Test

The Kakapo

The kakapo is a *rare* and strange parrot. It is the only parrot that can't fly. Although other parrots are active during the day, the kakapo parrot is *nocturnal.* It is also the largest and heaviest parrot.

Unfortunately, the kakapo is also the world's most *endangered* parrot. In 1999, there were only about 62 kakapo left on earth. This bird once was common *throughout* New Zealand. Now the last of these parrots have been put on six islands where they will be safe.

The kakapo became endangered because of human beings. People hunted them and chopped down the *forests* where they lived. They also brought *predators,* such as cats, rats, and dogs, that killed the kakapo easily. The kakapo were not afraid of the mammals because there had never been any on the islands. They did not know that they should either attack or *retreat.*

It was also bad luck for the kakapo that people liked their feathers and meat. The feathers were used to make clothing and to fill mattresses and pillows. Their meat was found to be *tasty.* Thousands were *slaughtered* and eaten. By the 1930s, the kakapo was *extinct* on the North Island of New Zealand.

I.

Circle the letter of the correct answer.

1. Which of the following words can replace *rare*?

    (a) usual   **(c)** beautiful

    (b) uncommon   **(d)** important

2. A *nocturnal* animal is active _____

    (a) during the day.   **(c)** at night.

    (b) all the time.   **(d)** sometimes.

3. The word *endangered* means _____

    (a) in trouble.   **(c)** healthy.

    (b) safe.   **(d)** lucky.

4. *Throughout* can be replaced with _____

    (a) at.   **(c)** above.

    (b) all over.   **(d)** around.

5. A *forest* is full of _____

    (a) houses.   **(c)** roads.

    (b) trees.   **(d)** spirits.

6. *Predators* were other animals that _____ the kakapo.

    (a) played with   **(c)** hunted

    (b) lived with   **(d)** frightened

7. The word *retreat* means _____

    (a) leave.   **(c)** accept.

    (b) approach.   **(d)** invite.

8. When animals are *slaughtered* they are killed _____

    (a) at night.   **(c)** for fun.

    (b) in great numbers.   **(d)** a little.

9. Something that is *tasty* is _____

    (a) delicious.   **(c)** unpleasant.

    (b) disgusting.   **(d)** sour.

10. *Extinct* means that there are _____ of a kind of animal.

    (a) lots   **(c)** no more

    (b) plenty   **(d)** a few more

II.

Circle the word in each group that does not belong.

1.	wanderer	tribe	traveler	nomad
2.	gather	collect	pick	buy
3.	fight	join	battle	resist
4.	custom	vacation	habit	tradition
5.	holiday	party	exam	celebration

■■■ Chapter 2 ■■■

Roots

Many of the words we use are formed using *roots*. We can figure out the definitions of words by looking for these roots and thinking about their meanings. Learning word roots is one of the easiest and most effective ways of increasing your vocabulary. You will be surprised at how many roots you already know. In this chapter, we will discuss some of the most common roots.

Reading Practice

Eclipses

What did ancient people think when the sky became dark and the sun disappeared? Was this incredible spectacle beautiful or frightening? From the information we have, it seems that eclipses terrified most people.

People believed that eclipses brought bad luck and destruction. The Babylonians thought that an eclipse meant that a terrible disaster would occur. The early Chinese believed that a solar eclipse was caused by a dragon trying to eat the sun. They would beat on drums and shoot arrows into the sky to chase it away. The Incas and people in India shared the same belief. The Incas also tried to scare away the monster that was eating the sun. People in India submerged themselves in water. This was a religious act. They thought it would help the sun fight the dragon.

It is not surprising that people were frightened when the sun was "eaten." Most cultures believed that the sun was beneficial and a source of life. Its disappearance was seen as an evil omen.

Exercise 1

Work with a partner, with a group, or alone to answer these questions. Use your dictionary.

1. The word root *cred* means "to believe." What do you think the connection is between *cred* and *incredible*?

    _____

    _____

2. The word root *spect* means "to look." Find a word in the passage with this root. What does it mean? Think of two more words that share this word root.

    _____

    _____

3. Do you think the word root *bene* means good or bad? Find a word in the passage that begins with *bene*. Find another one in your dictionary.

    _____

    _____

Exercise 2

A. Work with a partner, with a group, or alone. Read the roots in the box and then underline them in each sentence.

cred	bene	dict	vis/vid	spec

1. Try to visualize a solar eclipse if you have never seen one.

2. Some ancient rulers were benevolent dictators.

3. No one was able to predict when the next solar eclipse would occur.

4. When they shot arrows in the air, it was an incredible spectacle.

5. The sun was not visible for several hours.

B. These roots have the following meanings:

cred	=	to believe
bene	=	good, well
spec	=	to look
vid, vis	=	to see
dic, dict	=	to say

PRACTICE *Vocabulary*

How are these roots connected to the meanings of the words you underlined?
You may use your dictionaries.

_____

_____

_____

_____

_____

Strategies

- Most word roots are not used alone. They may have prefixes or suffixes attached to them.

    Example: The root *dict*, "to say or to speak," is never used alone. *Prefixes* like *pre-* or *contra-* (*predict, contradict*) or *suffixes* like *–ation* or *–ator* (*dictation, dictator*) are added to it.

- At first you may not see how a particular word was formed from the word root. Look at the word carefully. You will see the connection.

    Example: Look at the word *revolve*. It comes from the root *volv* which means "to turn" or "to roll." You can see the connection between the word *revolve* and the idea of turning or rolling.

- Once you recognize word roots, you will see the connection between many words. This will make it easier for you to understand new words and remember their meanings.

- Study the word roots in this chapter over a period of weeks. Try to learn a few each day. Review the roots you've learned. Try to use them in speaking and writing.

- Every time you look up a word in the dictionary, look at its root. Most words in English have Latin or Greek roots. Keep a list of new roots that you want to learn.

Root: *bio*

---

bio ¢ **life**

biological = having to do with living things

    Example: Bacteria are used in biological warfare.

biography = the history of a person's life written by someone else

    Example: You must read Simon Bolívar's biography to understand the history of South America.

biodegradable = able to be broken down by nature

    Example: Products that are not biodegradable hurt the environment.

symbiosis = a close relationship between living things which is usually beneficial

    Example: Honeypot ants and aphids have a symbiotic relationship.

autobiography = the story of a person's life written by that person

    Example: It is silly to write your autobiography before you grow old.

Exercise 3

Complete each sentence with one of the following words. Write your answer on the blank line.

biological	biography	biodegradable	symbiosis	autobiography

1. I will write my _____ when I am seventy years old.

2. Without _____, many species would not be able to survive.

3. Plastic bags are not _____, but paper bags are.

4. You must do a lot of research to write a/an _____.

5. We need _____ specimens to decide if the plants are related.

Exercise 4

Circle the letter of the correct word to complete each sentence.

1. _____ clocks help organisms live in harmony with nature.

    (a) Biological   **(b)** Biographical

2. Lichen, which is made up of algae and fungi living together, is an example of _____

    (a) biodegradable.   **(b)** symbiosis.

3. If you write the story of your own life, it is a/an _____

    (a) biography.   **(b)** autobiography.

4. Soaps that are _____ don't hurt the environment.

    (a) biographical   **(b)** biodegradable

5. It would be interesting to write a _____ of the life of Martin Luther King, Jr.

    (a) biography   **(b)** biological

Root: *cycl*

---

cycl ¢ **wheel, circle**

cyclist = a person who rides a bicycle or motorcycle

> *Example:* A cyclist has to watch out for traffic

cycle = an event that changes and repeats

> *Example:* The seasons are cycles of weather patterns.

cyclone = a violent rotating storm

> *Example:* Cyclones may be violent tropical storms.

recycle = to reuse materials

> *Example:* Steel is a material that is often recycled.

bicycle = a lightweight vehicle on two wheels that is moved by pedaling

> *Example:* The first bicycle was developed in France in the late 1600s.

Exercise 5

Match the words in Column B with their definitions in Column A. Write the letter of the word on the blank line.

Column A	Column B
_____ **1.** a two-wheeled vehicle	**(a)** cyclone
_____ **2.** to reuse materials	**(b)** cyclist
_____ **3.** an event that repeats itself	**(c)** bicycle
_____ **4.** a person who rides a two-wheeled vehicle	**(d)** cycle
_____ **5.** a violent storm	**(e)** recycle

PRACTICE *Vocabulary*

Exercise 6

Circle the letter of the correct word to complete each sentence.

1. I always try to buy products packed in _____ containers.

    (a) recycle   **(b)** recyclable

2. War and peace seem to be _____

    (a) cyclical.   **(b)** cycle.

3. Although they are hard to predict, _____ are visible before they touch the ground.

    (a) cyclones   **(b)** cyclists

4. Sometimes it's hard to see _____ at night.

    (a) cyclists   **(b)** cyclical

5. A vehicle with two wheels is called a _____

    (a) tricycle.   **(b)** bicycle.

Root: *spect, spec*

---

spect, spec ¢ **to look, watch**

spectacle = a strange or amazing sight

> *Example:* It was quite a spectacle when they shot the fireworks in the air.

specimen = a sample; something that is tested or shown

> *Example:* A specimen of moon rock was tested for minerals.

perspective = a way of looking at or judging something

> *Example:* Farmers look at seasons from a different perspective than do doctors.

retrospect = a look back at the past

> *Example:* In retrospect, we might do many things differently.

aspect = point of view

> *Example:* We studied different aspects of life in the United States.

Exercise 7

Replace the underlined words in the sentence with a word from the box. Cross out the underlined word or words and write the new word above.

aspect	spectacle	specimen	perspective	retrospect

1. In <u>looking at the past</u>, I should have studied physics in high school.

2. Whether you like or dislike modern art depends on your <u>way of looking at it</u>.

3. The doctor took a <u>sample</u> of blood to be analyzed.

4. Watching the northern lights in Alaska was quite a <u>strange or amazing sight</u>.

5. Having to earn money is just one <u>side</u> of modern life.

Exercise 8

The word with the *spec* root in each sentence is not correct. Cross it out and write the correct word above it. Make the necessary changes to the articles.

1. A perspective is a sample of something.

2. A strange or amazing sight is a specimen.

3. Retrospect is the way things are looked at or judged.

4. A specimen is one point of view.

5. Respected means looking back at the past.

Root: ced, cess

***ced, cess* ¢ to go, move along**

procedure = a detailed method of doing something

> *Example:* Most experiments follow an exact procedure.

precedent = a past action or case that sets an example or rule for the future

> *Example:* Most judges try to follow precedents when they make their rulings.

to recede = to move back or shrink in size

> *Example:* If your gums recede, you should see a dentist immediately.

to process = to apply a procedure to something

> *Example:* Photographic film has to be processed before we get the pictures.

to concede = to give victory or possession to someone else

> *Example:* We conceded victory to the visiting team when we knew we couldn't win.

Exercise 9

Complete each sentence with one of the following words. Write your answer on the blank line.

procedure	precedent	recede	process	concede

1. A _____ is a past action that sets an example for the future.

2. To _____ is to move back.

3. The loser has to _____ to the winner.

4. It can take several weeks to _____ a passport application.

5. A _____ is a particular system for doing something.

Exercise 10

Circle the letter of the correct word to complete each sentence.

1. As far as we know, there is no _____ for a mouse killing a tiger.

   (a) precedent   **(b)** process

2. It will take six months to _____ your request for a permit.

   (a) procedure   **(b)** process

3. I have to _____ that you know more about astronomy than I do.

   (a) concede   **(b)** recede

4. His hairline seems to _____ more each day.

   (a) recede   **(b)** concede

5. I am not sure about the _____ I have to follow in this experiment.

   (a) process   **(b)** procedure

Root: *duc, duct*

---

duc, duct ¢ **to lead**

to induce = to cause an effect

    Example: The poor living conditions induced many people to leave the
        country.

ductile = flexible, easily influenced

    Example: Copper wire is a ductile metal.

duct = a tube or canal that carries fluids, electric power, or telephone cables

    Example: Most glands in our body have ducts to carry their secretions.

to conduct = to lead

    Example: The visitor was conducted on a tour of the school.

to deduct = to subtract, or take away

    Example: He was surprised at how much was deducted from his paycheck for
        taxes.

Exercise 11

Match the words in *Column A* with their definitions in *Column B*. Write the letter of the definition on the blank line.

Column A	Column B
_____ 1. duct	**(a)** flexible
_____ 2. ductile	**(b)** a tube or canal
_____ 3. to conduct	**(c)** to take away
_____ 4. to deduct	**(d)** to cause an effect
_____ 5. to induce	**(e)** to lead

                PRACTICE *Vocabulary*

Exercise 12

Circle the letter of the correct word to complete each sentence.

1. Our new puppy has a very _____ personality and will be easy to train.

    (a) ductile   **(b)** conduct

2. The waiter _____ the guests to their table.

    (a) deducted   **(b)** conducted

3. Electrical wires have to be run inside a _____ when they are used outside a building.

    (a) duct   **(b)** ductile

4. The bank always _____ a service charge from my account.

    (a) conducts   **(b)** deducts

5. No one knows what _____ him to give his money to charity.

    (a) conducted   **(b)** induced

Exercise 13

You will find that the more roots you know, the more words you will be able to understand without using your dictionary.

Work with a partner or a group. Write down two examples of words for each root below. The area of meaning is given to help you. Use your dictionary to check your words.

Root	Area of Meaning	Examples	
agr	land	_____	_____
amb(u)l	walk	_____	_____
anima	life, spirit	_____	_____
anthro	man, mankind	_____	_____
aster	star	_____	_____
auto	self	_____	_____
bene	well, good	_____	_____
bibl	book	_____	_____
bio	life	_____	_____
brevi	short	_____	_____
capit	head	_____	_____
carn	flesh	_____	_____
ced, cess	go	_____	_____
cide	kill	_____	_____
civ	citizen	_____	_____
chron	time	_____	_____
corp	body	_____	_____
cosm	world, order	_____	_____
cred	believe	_____	_____
cycl	wheel, circle	_____	_____
demo	people	_____	_____
dic, dict	say, speak	_____	_____

domin	master	_____	_____
duc, duct	lead	_____	_____
dynam	power	_____	_____
fac, fact	do, make	_____	_____
flex	bend	_____	_____
form	shape	_____	_____
fort	strong	_____	_____
gamy	marriage	_____	_____
gen	birth	_____	_____
geo	earth	_____	_____
graph, gram	write	_____	_____

Exercise 14

Work with a partner or a group. Write down two examples of words for each root below. The area of meaning is given to help you. Use your dictionary to check your words.

Root	Area of Meaning	Examples	
hetero	other, different	_____	_____
homo	same	_____	_____
hydro	water	_____	_____
leg	law	_____	_____
loc	place	_____	_____
log, logy	speech, study, word	_____	_____
man, manu	hand	_____	_____
mar	sea	_____	_____
mater, matri	mother	_____	_____
medi	middle	_____	_____
mob	move	_____	_____
nom	name	_____	_____

Root	Area of Meaning	Examples	
omni	all	_____	_____
pater, patri	father	_____	_____
pathy	feeling	_____	_____
phon, phone	sound	_____	_____
port	carry	_____	_____
rupt	break	_____	_____
scope	watch	_____	_____
scrib, script	write	_____	_____
spect	look, watch	_____	_____
tax, tact	arrange, order	_____	_____
term	end, limit	_____	_____
theo	god	_____	_____
tract	draw, pull	_____	_____
urb	city	_____	_____
vene, vent	come, go	_____	_____
vid, vis	see	_____	_____
voc, vok	call	_____	_____
volu, volv	turn	_____	_____

End of Chapter Test

Illuminated Manuscripts

Manuscripts that are decorated are called *illuminated manuscripts.* The first illuminated manuscripts were made in Egypt. Copies of the "Book of the Dead" were decorated with pictures of gods, animals, and people. The manuscripts contained *descriptions* of ceremonies *preceding* burials, and prayers for the dead. They also *dictated* how the dead should behave in the afterlife.

During the Middle Ages in Europe, monks made most of the illuminated manuscripts. Many of them were decorated with gold and silver. Preparing a manuscript was a very difficult *process. Manufacturing* the paints was complicated. It took time and patience.

Scribes copied Middle Eastern manuscripts in the thirteenth and fourteenth centuries. They were decorated with beautiful designs in a *spectrum* of brilliant colors. Sometimes the designs *resembled* the patterns found on carpets. The people of ancient Palestine and Syria wrote on pieces of leather. Some manuscripts were written on thin sheets of copper. The copper was *flexible* enough to roll up. This made the manuscripts *portable.*

I.

Find the roots of the words in italics and then answer the questions.

1. What is a *manuscript*?

   _____

2. What does the word *descriptions* mean?

   _____

3. What is the meaning of the word *preceding*?

   _____

4. When you *dictate* something, what are you doing?

   _____

5. Explain what a *process* is.

   _____

6. What is another word for *manufacturing*?

   _____

7. What is a synonym for *spectrum*?

_____

8. What does the word *resembled* mean?

_____

9. What is an antonym for *flexible*?

_____

10. If something is *portable*, what can you do with it?

_____

II.

Use your dictionary and your knowledge of roots to answer these questions.

1. What does an *anthropologist* study?

_____

2. What do we call events in order of *time*?

_____

3. What does the word *immobilize* mean?

_____

4. What do we call a person who loves *books*?

_____

5. If something is *omnipresent*, where is it?

_____

■■■ Chapter 3 ■■■
Prefixes

A *prefix* is added in front of a word or word root to change its meaning. In fact, the *pre-* in *prefix* is a prefix that means "before." Learning prefixes will help you work out the meanings of words.

There are more than fifty prefixes in English, and you will work with most of them in this section. You will learn how to recognize them and use them to understand new words.

Reading Practice

The Bermuda Triangle

When Christopher Columbus passed through the Bermuda Triangle, he said that his compass did not work and he saw lights in the sky. Since then, more than a hundred boats, ships, and planes have mysteriously disappeared in the Triangle.

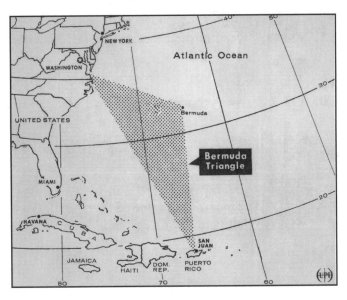

Are these unexplained disappearances related? No scientific evidence exists to prove this. Still, many sailors and pilots refer to the area as "The Devil's Triangle" or "The Triangle of Death."

The Bermuda Triangle is in the North Atlantic Ocean. It runs from Florida through Puerto Rico and Bermuda, then back to Florida. Pilots have reported that their instruments stop working or act abnormally in the Triangle. This can disorient and confuse them. Some have seen balls of light flying near their planes.

Scientists have different theories about the Bermuda Triangle. They propose that inadequate equipment, inclement weather, and inexperienced pilots were probably responsible for many accidents. Perhaps the lost ships are simply submerged and covered with sand.

Is there a black hole that sucks in airplanes? Are there magnets at the bottom of the sea that interrupt ships' progress? Is it possible that so many disappearances are coincidental? So far, no one has been able to explain the mystery of the Bermuda Triangle.

Exercise 1

Work with a partner, with a group, or alone to answer these questions. You may use your dictionary.

1. The word *appear* means to become visible or show up. What does *disappear* mean? What do you think the prefix *dis-* means?

   _____

2. Find another word in the passage that begins with the prefix *dis-*. What does it mean?

   _____

3. Find the word that begins with the prefix *un-*. What does this prefix mean?

   _____

4. Find three words in the passage that begin with the prefix *in-*. What do you think *in-* means?

   _____

   _____

5. Find the word in the passage that begins with *co-* . What does it mean?

   _____

6. List five words that begin with *co-*. You can use a dictionary.

   _____

   _____

7. One of the meanings of *pro-* is "forward." Give an example of a word in the passage that begins with *pro-* and refers to movement forward.

   _____

8. Use your dictionary to find three words that begin with *pro-*.

   _____

9. Find the word in the passage that begins with *sub-*. What does this prefix mean?

   _____

10 Find two words in the passage that begin with *re-*. What does *re-* mean?

   _____

Exercise 2

Complete each word, using the correct prefix. Write the prefix on the blank line. You may use the same prefix more than once.

dis-	re-	un-	in-	co-

1. Many sailors _____fuse to sail in the Bermuda Triangle.

2. Sometimes the weather is too _____pleasant to go outside.

3. No one can _____prove the theories about the Triangle.

4. It is very _____safe to travel with poor equipment.

5. I _____trust stories that suggest supernatural explanations for the accidents.

6. It is _____conceivable that such a place exists.

7. The pilots will _____operate with the investigation.

8. Your _____ply was interesting but wrong.

9. If you _____state your complaint, I will help you.

10. The _____pilot flies the plane when the pilot can't.

Strategies

■ Complete all of the exercises in this section. This will help you become familiar with the most common English prefixes. You will be able to recognize or guess what hundreds of words mean.

■ A prefix usually changes the meaning of a word. For example, the prefix *in-* changes the meaning of a word to the opposite. *Capable* means "having the ability of doing or being." *Incapable* means "not having the ability of doing or being."

■ Prefixes are often attached to roots of words. By knowing the prefix and root, you can work out the meaning of the words.

Examples: re ¢ tract
dis ¢ tract
pro ¢ tract

Prefix: de-

de- ¢ down, reversing, away from

to degenerate = to go down to a lower condition
>   *Example:* The argument degenerated into a fight.

to defer = to put off to a later time
>   *Example:* We deferred the decision until we could get more information.

to deplete = to reduce greatly
>   *Example:* The drought depleted the water supply.

to delete = to take out
>   *Example:* I deleted the paragraph about space aliens causing the accidents.

to defy = to oppose openly, refuse to obey
>   *Example:* It is dangerous to defy authority.

to detect = to uncover, find
>   *Example:* We detected lead in the paint.

to deport = to force someone, usually a foreigner, to leave a country
>   *Example:* The Japanese government deported the spy.

to descend = to go down
>   *Example:* The plane descended before it should have.

to detach = to remove, separate, or disconnect
>   *Example:* Don't detach the label from the pillow.

to deprive = to take something away from
>   *Example:* A bad government deprives people of their rights.

PRACTICE *Vocabulary*

Exercise 3

Circle T if the sentence is TRUE, or F if the sentence is FALSE.

1. To degenerate means to lower the condition.   T   F

2. To deplete means to reduce greatly.   T   F

3. To defer means to separate or disconnect.   T   F

4. To defy means to go down.   T   F

5. If you detect something, you discover or find it.   T   F

6. If you are told to detach something, you should put it down.   T   F

7. To deprive means to take something away.   T   F

8. When you descend, you stop something from happening.   T   F

9. To deport means to force to leave a country.   T   F

10. If you defer a decision, you reduce it.   T   F

Exercise 4

Complete each sentence with one of the following words. Write the word on the blank line. Change the verb form if necessary.

degenerate	defer	deplete	delay	defy
deport	descend	detach	deprive	detect

1. The ozone layer is _____ by certain types of pollution.

2. If you are a spy, you can be _____.

3. Don't _____ yourself of a college education.

4. _____ the mountain carefully.

5. The quality of his paintings started out good, but then it

 _____.

6. We were able to _____ the cabinet from the wall.

7. You can _____ osteoporosis by getting enough calcium.

8. The trip has been _____ until after the rainy season.

9. Without a microscope, it is impossible to _____ microbes.

10. When he _____ the general's orders, he knew he would be punished.

Prefix: *inter-*

inter- ¢ **between, among**

intermittent = stopping for a time and then continuing

>   *Example:* The rain was not continuous but intermittent.

intermediate = in the middle level, between two extremes

>   *Example:* The intermediate level is perfect for you because you are neither a beginner nor an advanced student.

to intervene = to interrupt something, usually to stop something bad from happening

>   *Example:* The police intervened before they started fighting.

interdependent = needing something from someone or something that needs something in return

>   *Example:* Flowers and honeybees are interdependent.

to interfere = to enter or interrupt a situation or discussion, usually without permission

>   *Example:* Sometimes, when you think you know what is right, it is hard not to interfere.

intermission = the time between acts (of a play or other performance)

>   *Example:* I bought popcorn during intermission.

to interact = to communicate with someone

>   *Example:* The play was a success because of the way the actors interacted with each other.

to interrelate = to connect to one another

>   *Example:* Reading and writing skills are interrelated.

to intercept = to catch or stop on the way

>   *Example:* The guards intercepted the prisoner as he was climbing out of the window.

intersection = a place where roads cross

>   *Example:* The traffic is terrible at the intersection of Main Street and First Avenue.

Exercise 5

Circle T if the sentence is TRUE, or F if the sentence is FALSE.

1. Something that is intermittent stops and then starts again.   T   F

2. Intermission is the period between school semesters.   T   F

3. If two countries' economies are interrelated, they are somehow   T   F
   connected to each other.

4. If something is intercepted, it is forbidden by law.   T   F

5. To interact is to act between two events.   T   F

6. An intersection is a place where roads cross.   T   F

7. Intermediate is the level in the middle.   T   F

8. To interfere is to ask for assistance.   T   F

9. When you intervene, you usually are trying to stop something   T   F
   bad from happening.

10. When interdependent plants are separated, they may die.   T   F

Exercise 6

Complete each sentence with one of the following words. Write the word on the blank line. Change the word form if necessary.

intermittent	intervene	intermediate	interdependent	interfere
intermission	interact	interrelate	intercept	intersection

1. The snow was _____ all day.

2. The students were divided into three groups: beginning, _____,
   and advanced.

3. If you need to make a phone call during the play, try to make it during

   _____.

4. When it was clear that the student might fail, the teachers decided to

   _____.

5. The police _____ the speeding motorist at a road block.

6. Sometimes young children don't know how to _____ with each
   other.

7. In economics, supply and demand are _____.

8. Most parents try not to _____ in their children's lives.

9. Species that are _____ cannot live if they are separated.

10. Some cities have particularly dangerous _____ where there are
    many traffic accidents.

Copyright © 2002 Heinle & Heinle

Prefix: *pro-*

---

pro- ¢ **before, in favor of, forward**

to promote = to advance in rank

> *Example:* To be promoted, you must pass the final exam.

to proliferate = to reproduce and increase in number

> *Example:* Rabbits and other rodents proliferate quickly.

to protrude = to stick out

> *Example:* The house was designed to protrude over the water.

profound = intellectually deep

> *Example:* Gandhi had a profound understanding of human nature.

to proclaim = to declare or say in public

> *Example:* When the colonists proclaimed their independence, they knew it
> would lead to war.

proficient = very skilled or expert

> *Example:* He is a proficient cook.

prominent = well-known and respected

> *Example:* She is a prominent lawyer in this community.

profuse = abundant or plentiful

> *Example:* He gave her profuse thanks for saving his life.

prospective = expected or future

> *Example:* The prospective patient wanted to know where the doctor had
> studied.

to protect = to defend against harm or loss

> *Example:* It is important to use sun block to protect your skin from harmful
> radiation.

Exercise 7

Match the word in the box with its definition on the next page. Write the word on the
blank line next to its definition.

promote	proliferate	protrude	profound	proclaim
proficient	prominent	profuse	prospective	protect

Copyright © 2002 Heinle & Heinle

1. deep _____

2. reproduce _____

3. defend _____

4. expert in _____

5. announce in public _____

6. stick out _____

7. expected _____

8. well-known _____

9. raise in rank _____

10. abundant _____

Exercise 8

Complete each sentence with one of the words on the opposite page that begin with the prefix *pro-*. Change the verb form if necessary.

1. My sister was just _____ to captain.

2. His writings were so _____, they have been studied for centuries.

3. Sailors must be careful of rocks that _____ near the dock.

4. The virus _____ so quickly, it is hard to control.

5. Abraham Lincoln _____ that all men and women were free.

6. Despite her _____ apologies for the poor service, we will not return.

7. He is known and respected as one of the most _____ doctors in the city.

8. Certain products have been banned in order to _____ the environment.

9. _____ students should research their courses before they register.

10. Joseph Conrad was born in Poland, but was so _____ in English that he is considered to be one of the greatest modern English-language writers.

Prefix: *dis-*

dis- ¢ reverse, undo, negate

to discard = to throw away

> *Example:* It is important to discard medicine that has expired.

to disintegrate = to break down into small pieces

> *Example:* When asbestos disintegrates, it becomes a health hazard.

to disorient = to cause someone to lose his or her sense of direction or time

> *Example:* Some pilots become disoriented in the Bermuda Triangle.

to dissuade = to persuade or advise someone not to do something

> *Example:* She tried to dissuade people from wearing fur coats.

to dispense = to distribute or give out

> *Example:* After the earthquake, volunteers dispensed water and food.

to disprove = to prove false

> *Example:* Copernicus disproved the theory that all planets move around the Earth.

to dissolve = to change into liquid

> *Example:* The cocoa dissolved in the milk.

disposable = meant to be thrown away after use

> *Example:* Today, most medical supplies are disposable.

to dissatisfy = to not satisfy or not please

> *Example:* Sailors are dissatisfied with the explanations they have heard for the disappearances.

to disrupt = to disturb or interrupt

> *Example:* The protestors disrupted the meeting.

Exercise 9

Circle T if the sentence is TRUE, or F if the sentence is FALSE.

1. If you want to stop someone from doing something, try   T   F
    to dissuade him or her.

2. You disprove something you don't like.   T   F

3. When you are disoriented, you may lose your sense of direction.   T   F

4. When something disintegrates, it falls to pieces.   T   F

5. When you discard something, you save it.   T   F

6. When something is dissolved, it keeps its shape.   T   F

7. Something disposable can be thrown away after being used. T   F

8. When you are dissatisfied, you are pleased.   T   F

9. To dispense something means to throw it away.   T   F

10. When you disrupt something, you interrupt it.   T   F

Exercise 10

Complete each sentence with one of the following words. Write the word on the blank line.
Change the verb form if necessary.

discard	disintegrate	disorient	dissuade	dispense
disprove	dissolve	disposable	disrupt	dissatisfy

1. His parents tried to _____ him from dropping out
    of school.

2. After a severe accident, you may feel _____ for a while.

3. Mothers and babies are grateful that _____ diapers were
    invented.

4. If no one can _____ a theory, it is accepted as reliable.

5. Some clinics _____ free medicine to patients who can't
    afford to buy it.

6. Some recipes tell you to _____ sugar in hot water.

7. It seems that some customers are always _____, no
    matter how hard you try to please them.

8. It is very rude to _____ a person's meal.

9. You should immediately _____ mayonnaise that has been
    left in the sun.

10. Rusted metal may _____ when you touch it.

Other Prefixes

The following prefixes are used in many words. By learning them, you will increase your ability to understand new words.

Exercise 11

Work with a partner or a group. Write down two examples of words for each prefix below. The area of meaning is given to help you. Use your dictionary to check your words.

Prefix	Area of Meaning	Examples	
ambi-	both	_____	_____
ante-	before	_____	_____
anti-	against, opposite	_____	_____
auto-	self	_____	_____
bi-	two	_____	_____
circum-	around	_____	_____
co-	with, together	_____	_____
counter-	in opposition to	_____	_____
de-	down, out	_____	_____
dec-	ten	_____	_____
demi-	half	_____	_____
dis-	not, bad	_____	_____
ex-, e-	out of, from	_____	_____
extra-	beyond	_____	_____
hemi-	half	_____	_____
hyper-	beyond	_____	_____
in-, ir-	not	_____	_____
inter-	between	_____	_____
macro-	large	_____	_____
mal-	bad	_____	_____
micro-	small	_____	_____

Prefix	Area of Meaning	Examples	
mini-	little, small	_____	_____
mis-	wrong	_____	_____
mono-	one	_____	_____
multi-	many	_____	_____
non-	no, not	_____	_____

Exercise 12

Work with a partner or a group. Write down two examples of words for each prefix below. The area of meaning is given to help you. Use your dictionary to check your words.

Prefix	Area of Meaning	Examples	
over-	too much	_____	_____
pan-	all	_____	_____
poly-	many	_____	_____
post-	after, behind	_____	_____
pre-	before	_____	_____
pro-	for, on the side of	_____	_____
re-	again, back	_____	_____
semi-	half	_____	_____
sub-	under	_____	_____
super-	above, more than	_____	_____
syn-	with, at the same time	_____	_____
trans-	across	_____	_____
tri-	three	_____	_____
ultra-	beyond	_____	_____
under-	not enough	_____	_____
uni-	one, single	_____	_____
vice-	deputy	_____	_____

End of Chapter Test

I.

Use one of the prefixes in the box to give the adjective its *opposite* meaning. Write the prefix on the blank line.

ir- il- im- in- dis- un-

1. an _____polite person

2. an _____relevant question

3. a _____oriented person

4. an _____legible letter

5. an _____curable disease

6. an _____familiar place

7. an _____trustworthy friend

8. _____mature behavior

9. an _____impressive performance

10. an _____expensive restaurant

II.

Circle the letter of the answer that could best replace the underlined word. Your choice should not change the meaning of the sentence.

1. Ultrasonic waves can <u>detect</u> cracks in metal that the human eye cannot see.

   (a) stop

   (b) find

   (c) arrange

   (d) mend

2. The <u>profuse</u> tropical forests of the Amazon are inhabited by different kinds of animals.

   (a) wild

   (b) distant

   (c) abundant

   (d) immersed

3. When a person has a high fever, <u>disorientation</u> may occur.

   (a) disposition

   (b) confusion

   (c) complication

   (d) depression

4. A government's economic resources should not be <u>depleted</u>.

   (a) wasted

   (b) greatly reduced

   (c) badly destroyed

   (d) disorganized

5. German astronomer Johannes Kepler <u>disproved</u> Pythagorus's theory that the Earth was the center of the universe.

   (a) praised

   (b) confirmed

   (c) denied

   (d) demonstrated

PRACTICE *Vocabulary*

6. Oil and gas were formed from the <u>decomposed</u> bodies of creatures that died millions of years ago.

    (a) broken up   **(c)** solid

    (b) detached   **(d)** combined

7. James McNeill Whistler <u>promoted</u> the idea of art for art's sake.

    (a) put forward   **(c)** fought

    (b) disproved   **(d)** acquired

8. Bacteria often reproduce through <u>binary</u> fission (splitting).

    (a) single   **(c)** multiple

    (b) double   **(d)** triple

9. Cesar Chavez was the most <u>prominent</u> member of the United Farm Workers Union.

    (a) important   **(c)** interesting

    (b) dedicated   **(d)** active

10. A parrot fish is a <u>multicolored</u> tropical marine fish.

    (a) many colored   **(c)** spotted

    (b) monochromatic   **(d)** striped

▄▄▀ Chapter 4 ▀▄▄
Suffixes

A *suffix* is a combination of letters added to the end of a word or word root. Suffixes are used either to show the function of a word or to form new words. For example, the suffix *–ist* or *–ian* describes people, forming words like *motorist* and *musician*.

In this chapter you will learn some common suffixes that identify nouns, verbs, adjectives, and adverbs. You will learn to recognize errors in word forms and to use suffixes to develop your vocabulary.

Reading Practice

Elizabeth Blackwell (1821–1910)

Elizabeth Blackwell was born in Bristol, England. When she was eleven, her family moved to New York City, where she grew up. When Blackwell decided to become a doctor, she applied to medical schools in the Northeast. Twenty-nine medical schools turned her down. Still, she refused to give up. Finally, she was admitted to Geneva Medical School in Geneva, New York. Initially, students and teachers treated her with hostility. She eventually won their respect. When she graduated with honors in 1849, she became the first female physician in the United States.

Dr. Blackwell spent her entire life fighting intolerance and discrimination. For several years, she was unable to work because hospitals refused to hire her. Despite her excellent qualifications, she had almost no patients. No one would rent her space for an office, so she finally was forced to buy a house in a poor section of New York. This eventually became the New York Infirmary for Women and Children.

Her plans to open a women's medical college were delayed by the Civil War. In 1868, the Women's Medical College of the New York Infirmary was finally established. Elizabeth Blackwell is remembered for her great intelligence, her generosity, and her determination. As one of the first champions of women's rights, she opened the way for women in many different fields.

Exercise 1

Work with a partner, with a group, or alone to answer these questions.

1. **A.** Write three words that describe some of Elizabeth Blackwell's admirable qualities.

    _____

    B. Find one other word for each suffix on the words in part A. Look in a dictionary. Are the words you find nouns or adjectives?

    _____

2. **A.** What was Elizabeth Blackwell's profession?

    _____

    B. Write two other jobs with the same ending as the answer in part A. Are these words nouns or adjectives?

    _____

    _____

3. Find three adverbs of time in the passage.

    _____

    _____

4. **A.** What did Dr. Blackwell fight all of her life?

    _____

    _____

    B. Write two more words with the same endings as in part A. Are they nouns or adjectives?

    _____

    _____

5. **A.** Elizabeth Blackwell was a _____ of women's rights.

    B. Write two more words with the same ending as the answer in part A. Are they nouns or adjectives?

    _____

    _____

Strategies

- You do not have to know the meaning of a word to figure out what part of speech it is. You can recognize the distinctive forms of each word. Here is a nonsense sentence:

  Togonapism fotted isropation leposly.

  Although these words have no meanings, we can recognize the forms such as *-ism* and *-tion* as noun forms, *-ed* as a verb form, and *-ly* as an adverb.

- A common error involves the use of an adjective in place of an adverb, or an adverb in place of an adjective. Remember that adjectives usually answer the question *What kind?* Adjectives modify nouns, noun phrases, and pronouns.

  Example: Eleanor Roosevelt was an *influential* First Lady.

- Adverbs usually answer the question *How?* Adverbs modify verbs, adjectives, and participles. Most adverbs are formed by adding *-ly* to the adjective.

  Example: Theodore Roosevelt traveled *extensively*.

- Remember that some adjectives also end in *-ly*.

- Be careful not to confuse words related to certain fields and the people who work in the field (*botany* [the field], *botanical* [the adjective], *botanist* [the person]).

- Be careful not to confuse adjectives with nouns (*developing* [adjective], *development* [noun].)

- Remember not to confuse noun and verb forms (*belief* [noun], *believe* [verb]).

Noun Suffixes

These endings tell you that a word is a noun.

The following suffixes indicate people who do things:

Suffix	Examples
-ee	trainee, interviewee
-er	interviewer, employer
-or	translator, demonstrator

The following suffixes describe people:

Suffix	Examples
-an, -ian	Mexican, Parisian, historian
-ist	journalist, artist

Other noun suffixes:

Suffix	Examples
-age	passage, postage
-al	renewal, arrival
-ance, -ence	acceptance, independence
-dom	kingdom, freedom
-hood	childhood, motherhood
-ion, -sion, -tion	addition, conclusion, translation
-ism	materialism, realism
-y, -ity	prosperity, hostility
-ment	entertainment, employment
-ness	kindness, greatness
-ship	relationship, courtship
-sis	diagnosis
-ure	failure

Exercise 2

Change these verbs into nouns by adding the correct suffix. Write the noun on the blank line. You may use your dictionary if necessary.

1. use _____

2. close _____

3. assemble _____

4. encourage _____

5. try _____

6. exist _____

7. store _____

8. deny _____

9. produce _____

10. explode _____

Exercise 3

Circle the letter of the correct word to complete each sentence. Use your dictionary to help you.

1. His _____ was irritating.

   (a) insistence   **(b)** insistal

2. Recent advancements in communications are a great _____

   (a) improvement.   **(b)** improval.

3. What is your _____

   (a) preferage?   **(b)** preference?

4. The _____ of women from medicine lasted until the mid 1800s in the United States.

   (a) exclusism   **(b)** exclusion

5. A good _____ should be subtle but make its point.

   (a) advertisement   **(b)** advertisal

6. The _____ of property is not allowed in most states.

   (a) seizage   **(b)** seizure

7. She wanted to be a _____ but became a teacher instead.

   (a) translator   **(b)** translater

8. Her _____ of a house made the clinic possible.

   (a) acquisment   **(b)** acquisition

9. _____ was the goal of many territories.

   (a) Statedom   **(b)** Statehood

10. Small submarines made the _____ possible.

   (a) recovery   **(b)** recoverence

Adjective Suffixes

These endings tell you that a word is an adjective.

Suffix	Examples
-able, -ible	comparable, sensible
-ary	complimentary
-ative	formative
-ent	prudent
-ic	dramatic, democratic
-ical	musical, practical
-ish	childish
-ive	attractive, protective
-like	childlike, godlike
-ly	nightly, scholarly
-ory	sensory, satisfactory
-ous	poisonous, adventurous
-some	handsome, lonesome
-worthy	trustworthy
-y	salty, rainy

The suffixes *-ful* (with) and *-less* (without):

Suffix	Examples
-ful	faithful, hopeful
-less	helpless, careless

Comparatives and superlatives:

These endings are only for one-syllable adjectives. *More/less* and *most/least* are used with two- or more syllable adjectives.

Suffix	Examples
-er	smaller, longer
-est	widest, tallest

Exercise 4

Change the following words into adjectives by adding the correct suffix. Write the adjective on the blank line. You may use your dictionary if necessary.

1. week   _____

2. agree   _____

3. talk   _____

4. adjust   _____

5. inform   _____

6. humor   _____

7. courage   _____

8. tire   _____

9. pain   _____

10. poet   _____

Exercise 5

Circle the letter of the correct word to complete each sentence.

1. Exposure to _____ chemicals is bad for your health.

   (a) harmful   **(b)** harmly

2. Poor _____ conditions may have caused plants to disappear.

   (a) climatous   **(b)** climatic

3. Being an animal trainer is a _____ job.

   (a) dangerful   **(b)** dangerous

4. Some people find it difficult to put words into _____ order.

   (a) alphabeticous   **(b)** alphabetical

5. The baby choked on a _____ of cereal.

   (a) mouthful   **(b)** mouthsome

6. Despite his age, he kept his _____ appearance.

   (a) boyish   **(b)** boyful

7. The child made a _____ recovery.

   (a) miraclical   **(b)** miraculous

8. Cattle need a _____ place to graze.

   (a) grassy   **(b)** grassish

9. You need great _____ ability to be a set designer.

   (a) creatant   **(b)** creative

10. He is known to be a _____ student.

   (a) dependable   **(b)** dependworthy

Adverb Suffixes

These endings tell you that a word is an adverb. (The endings *-er* and *-est* are only used with one-syllable adverbs.)

Suffix	Examples
-ly	slowly, sharply
-er (comparative)	harder, faster
-est (superlative)	loudest, slowest

Verb Suffixes

These endings tell you that a word is a verb.

Suffix	Examples
-en	strengthen, weaken
-ate	activate, domesticate
-ize	sterilize, tranquilize
-fy, -ify	pacify, purify

Exercise 6

Change the following words into verbs by adding the correct suffix. In some cases you may have to change the spelling of the root word. Write the verb on the blank line. You may use your dictionary.

1. hospital _____

2. thick _____

3. captive _____

4. length _____

5. immune _____

6. regular _____

7. false _____

8. fright _____

9. liberty _____

10. dark _____

Exercise 7

Circle the letter of the correct word to complete each sentence.

1. They _____ the highway because of the increase in traffic.

   (a) broadened   **(b)** broadized

2. Ice is water in a _____ form.

   (a) solidated   **(b)** solidified

3. Sugar is used to _____ food.

   (a) sweetify   **(b)** sweeten

4. The police tried to _____ the angry mob.

   (a) pacify   **(b)** pacificate

5. It is important to _____ old mistakes.

   (a) rectify   **(b)** rectificate

6. Don't _____ about how people of different countries behave.

   (a) generalize   **(b)** generalate

7. The damage done to the environment can't be _____

   (a) quantified.   **(b)** quantificated.

8. Anyone who _____ should be admitted.

   (a) qualificates   **(b)** qualifies

9. The old wound seemed to have _____

   (a) deepened.   **(b)** deepated.

10. The sheriff _____ seven men to help him find the outlaw.

   (a) deputized   **(b)** depufied

End of Chapter Test

I.

Complete the chart with the correct word forms and suffixes. In some cases, there may be more than one answer. Follow the example.

	Verb	Noun	Adjective	Adverb
1.	beautify	beauty	beautiful	beautifully
2.		repetition		
3.			different	
4.				electrically
5.		emphasis		
6.			economical	
7.	decide			
8.		competition		
9.			exclusive	
10.				purely

II.

Complete the chart with the correct word forms. Follow the example.

	Thing	Person	Adjective
1.	art	artist	artistic
2.		politician	
3.			musical
4.	electricity		
5.	botany		

■■■ Chapter 5 ■■■

Words for Living Things

Another way of building your vocabulary is by grouping words with similar meanings under topics. If we look at the topic "Types of light," we can see that although there are several words that mean *to shine,* each one is a little bit different in intensity and use. The word *glisten* means *to shine* but is often used to describe things that are wet. *Twinkle* implies the light is unsteady and is often used to describe the stars or the light in a person's eyes.

This section features different themes with accompanying exercises. Since only a certain number of themes can be covered in this book, you should start to make lists of words under your own topics to continue to build your vocabulary.

Reading Practice

The Mystery of Popcorn

Who made the first popcorn? This is a mystery that will probably never be solved. It is likely that it was the Mexicans, since we know that corn appeared about 4,600 years ago in southern Mexico. We also know that it was grown in China, Sumatra, and India long before the first Europeans arrived in the Americas.

The first European settlers had a choice of hundreds of different types of popcorn. It was used to make a popular drink, for jewelry, to decorate headdresses, and in religious rituals. Of course it was also eaten in a variety of ways. Uses were found not only for the edible kernels, but also for the husks and the cobs.

American colonists ate their first popcorn at the first Thanksgiving feast. Today, North Americans eat more popcorn than anyone else. Over 450 million pounds of corn for popping are grown in the United States every year. But who discovered that corn kernels would expand and pop open when they were heated? We will probably never know.

Exercise 1

Work with a partner, with a group, or alone to answer the following questions. Write or say the answers. Use your dictionary.

1. What is a *husk*?

   _____

2. Name two things that have husks.

   _____

3. What is a *kernel*?

   _____

4. Who arrived in the Americas and found hundreds of varieties of popcorn?

   _____

5. What words do you know for people living in a country?

   _____

   _____

6. Are the people you mentioned in question 5 all *settlers*? Give reasons.

   _____

   _____

7. What is a *cob*?

   _____

8. What do you call a piece (not the individual kernels) of corn?

   _____

9. What parts of the corn are used?

   _____

10. Who made the first popcorn?

    _____

Conversation Practice

Read the following conversation.

Mike: Becca, I'd like you to meet my friend, Igor. He's an ***immigrant*** from Ukraine.

Becca: I'm so happy to meet you. Mike's told me so much about you.

Igor: I've heard a lot about you, too.

Becca: Do you like living in Los Angeles?

Igor: Very much. In fact, I already feel like a ***native***. I've even learned to surf.

Becca: That's great! What's that you're eating?

Igor: It's a pomegranate. Haven't you ever tried one?

Becca: No. I've seen them in the grocery store, but I never knew how to eat one.

Igor: I'll show you. You don't eat the rind. You just eat the ***flesh*** and the ***seeds.*** Try some. The seeds are very sweet. I'm sure you'll like it.

Becca: You're right. They're delicious. If I plant a seed, will it grow into a ***seedling***?

Igor: I don't know. It's worth trying.

Exercise 2

Work with a partner, with a group, or alone to answer the following questions.

1. Is Igor a *tourist*?

   _____

2. What is the difference between a *tourist* and an *immigrant*?

   _____

3. Find two other words for *friend*. Use your dictionary.

   _____

4. What parts of the pomegranate do you eat?

   _____

   _____

5. What is a *seedling*?

   _____

Strategies

- A good way of learning new vocabulary words is to include them in a group of words that have to do with a theme. If you include a word like *seedling* in a group called "Plants," you'll be able to distinguish it from other plant words like *sprout* and *shoot*.

- You may know or recognize some of the words in each topic. This will help you remember the new words.

- Use associations to remember slight differences in meaning. For example:
  sparkle – diamonds, glass, water
  glow – firelight, lights, candles

- Attach new words to one basic word that you already know. Here are some suggestions:
  seeing and *looking*
  rough and *coarse*
  good and *beneficial*
  damage and *destroy*

Types of Inhabitants

inhabitant = a person or animal that lives in one place, usually a country or a region, for a very long time

> *Example:* The only human inhabitants of the Gobi Desert were some nomadic tribes.

dweller = a person or animal that lives in a named place such as a cave, tree, or city

> *Example:* Most city dwellers get used to the high level of noise.

resident = a person who lives in a place and is not a visitor

> *Example:* Most residents of this neighborhood park their cars on the street.

pioneer = a person who is one of the first to come to an unknown place to live or work there

> *Example:* The American West was settled by pioneers in the 1800s.

native = a person, animal, or plant born or coming from a certain area

> *Example:* The koala bear is a native of Australia.

indigenous = originating and living in an area, native

> *Example:* Many indigenous people of Ecuador wear traditional clothing.

settler = a person who moves to a new country

> *Example:* The first settlers in America were the Pilgrims, who came from England.

colonist = a person who lives in a land that is governed by a different country

> *Example:* The early colonists faced many hardships in a new land.

immigrant = a person who moves permanently to a country. The first immigrants are called *settlers*.

> *Example:* Alexander Graham Bell, the inventor of the telephone, was an immigrant who came to America from Scotland.

Exercise 3

Circle T if the sentence is TRUE, or F if the sentence is FALSE.

1. A pioneer usually is the last to go to a new place.   T   F

2. The Aborigines, a group of people who have always lived in Australia, are indigenous to that country.   T   F

3. A native Californian is a person who was born in California.   T   F

4. A colonist is a person who lives in a cave or a tree.   T   F

5. Cave dwellers usually live in trees.   T   F

6. A resident is a person who comes to a new country to settle and live there.   T   F

7. A pioneer is a person who goes to an unknown land.   T   F

8. The most commonly known inhabitant of the North Pole is the polar bear.   T   F

9. European settlers came to live in America in the seventeenth century.   T   F

10. An immigrant has moved permanently to a new country.   T   F

Exercise 4

Circle the letter of the correct word or words to complete each sentence.

1. The Dutch who moved to South Africa were _____

   (a) colonists.   (b) natives.   (c) indigenous.

2. The orangutan, a large ape, is a _____ of Sumatra and Borneo.

   (a) pioneer   (b) native   (c) dweller

3. Levi Strauss, the man who invented blue jeans, was _____ to the United States.

   (a) an immigrant   (b) a settler   (c) an inhabitant

4. The Native Americans helped the first _____ from England to survive in a new land.

   (a) residents   (b) inhabitants   (c) settlers

5. Rumors of gold led some early _____ to the American West.

   (a) pioneers   (b) settlers   (c) dwellers

6. Dinosaurs were among the first _____ of the Earth.

   (a) immigrants   (b) inhabitants   (c) residents

The Life of Plants

seedling = a young plant grown from a seed

> **Example:** Ten days after the seeds were planted, the first seedlings appeared.

sprout = a new growth on a plant

> **Example:** These onions must be old; they have sprouts on them.

shoot = a new growth from a plant, such as a bush or tree

> **Example:** After the rose bush was cut back, new shoots started to grow.

bud = a flower or leaf that has not yet opened

> **Example:** When you buy roses, they are usually buds.

to blossom = to flower, usually used for fruit trees

> **Example:** In the spring, the cherry trees blossom.

to bloom or **to be in bloom** = to have flowers or to be in flower

> **Example:** The park is beautiful with the roses in bloom.

to wilt = to become limp or less fresh

> **Example:** In hot weather, most flowers begin to wilt because they need water.

to droop = to hang down

> **Example:** It was sad to see the sunflowers drooping toward the ground.

to wither = to dry up and die

> **Example:** I kept the flowers on the table until they withered.

Exercise 5

Circle T if the sentence is TRUE, or F if the sentence is FALSE.

1. A flower left without water will blossom.	T	F
2. When a flower droops, it does not stand up straight.	T	F
3. A withered fruit is usually not very appealing.	T	F
4. A seedling is so big it has to be tied to a stake.	T	F
5. A blossom may open up into a beautiful bud.	T	F
6. Sprouts on a plant mean it is growing.	T	F
7. New shoots mean that a plant is dying.	T	F
8. Too much heat and not enough water will cause flowers to wilt.	T	F
9. Fruit trees never blossom.	T	F
10. When a flower blooms, it becomes a seedling.	T	F

Exercise 6

Circle the letter of the correct word to complete each sentence.

1. When the orange trees _____, there is a sweet fragrance in the air.

   (a) droop   (b) blossom   (c) wither

2. The roses I left in the car started to _____ after a few hours in the heat.

   (a) wither   (b) blossom   (c) sprout

3. The tree has not grown very much in years, but this year, there is a new _____

   (a) shoot.   (b) bud.   (c) sprout.

4. After you plant your seeds, don't forget to water them or you won't see any _____

   (a) blooms.   (b) seedlings.   (c) buds.

5. The heads of the flowers were _____ after two weeks without water.

   (a) blooming   (b) wilting   (c) sprouting

6. If you keep potatoes in a warm place, they will grow _____

   (a) sprouts.   (b) seedlings.   (c) buds.

7. The hills look golden when the poppies are in _____

   (a) bud.   (b) bloom.   (c) blossom.

8. The vines got a strange disease, and the grapes started to _____

   (a) bloom.   (b) wither.   (c) blossom.

9. When we got the plant, we didn't know that the _____ would open into such beautiful flowers.

   (a) sprouts   (b) buds   (c) shoots

10. Each pink _____ on the cherry tree was a tiny work of art.

    (a) blossom   (b) sprout   (c) shoot

Parts of a Fruit or Nut

seed or **stone** or **pit** = the small inner hard part of a fruit that can grow into a small plant

Example: Cherries have hard pits.

kernel = the inside part of a fruit stone, or a nut

Example: The pistachio nut has a delicious green kernel.

peel = the outer covering of a fruit

Example: You cannot eat a banana with its peel on.

rind = the outer covering of certain fruits like oranges, lemons, or melons

Example: Orange and lemon rinds are often made into candy or marmalade.

skin = the thin outer coverings of fruit such as apples, plums, or peaches

Example: If you put peaches in boiling water, the skin will come off more easily.

husk = the dry outer covering of a fruit or nut

Example: You remove the husk from a coconut before eating it.

flesh = the soft substance of a fruit

Example: The peach has soft yellowish flesh.

shell = the hard outer covering of a fruit, nut, or egg

Example: Most common nuts, like hazelnuts, almonds, and walnuts, have shells.

Exercise 7

Circle T if the sentence is TRUE, or F if the sentence is FALSE.

		T	F
1.	The shell is the outer covering of an apple.	T	F
2.	The skin is a general word for a fruit.	T	F
3.	The peel is the outer covering of apples or pears.	T	F
4.	The husk is the dry outer covering of corn.	T	F
5.	The kernel is often made into candy or marmalade.	T	F
6.	Almonds have a soft peel.	T	F
7.	The rind is the outer covering of certain fruits such as oranges and lemons.	T	F
8.	Flesh is the soft juicy substance of fruit.	T	F
9.	The kernel is the most important part of an apple.	T	F

Exercise 8

Circle the letter of the correct word to complete each sentence.

1. The _____ is the part that can become a new plant.

   (a) husk   (b) stone   (c) kernel

2. After taking the outer covers off the corn, we were surrounded by a pile of _____

   (a) rinds.   (b) flesh.   (c) husks.

3. Some watermelons have hundreds of _____

   (a) seeds.   (b) shells.   (c) rinds.

4. Plums have hard _____

   (a) skin.   (b) flesh.   (c) stones.

5. The _____ of the avocado is delicious and rich.

   (a) skin   (b) flesh   (c) kernel

6. Lemon _____ is often used in cakes.

   (a) rind   (b) husk   (c) seed

7. The _____ of an egg is not good to eat.

   (a) peel   (b) husk   (c) shell

8. A brown _____ often shows that a piece of fruit is too old.

   (a) skin   (b) seed   (c) kernel

9. A banana _____ is usually yellow when the fruit is ripe.

   (a) flesh   (b) kernel   (c) peel

10. You can eat the _____ of a plum.

    (a) skin   (b) kernel   (c) husk

End of Chapter Test

I.

Complete each sentence with one of the following words. Write the word on the blank line.

wither	shell	native	rind	immigrant
kernel	blossom	pioneer	droop	pit

1. A person who comes to a country to make a new home is

   a/an _____.

2. The hard covering of a nut is called the _____.

3. To _____ means to dry up and/or become smaller in size.

4. The part of the corn that you pop is called the _____.

5. The outer covering of certain fruits like lemons and oranges is

   the _____.

6. When fruit trees _____, they flower.

7. A heavy flower won't _____ if you tie it to a post.

8. The quetzal is _____ to Central America.

9. The stone of a fruit is the same thing as the _____.

10. A person who is first to discover something and lead the way for others can

    be called a _____ in his or her field.

II.

Circle the letter of the answer that could best replace the underlined word. Your choice should not change the meaning of the sentence.

1. A coconut palm's <u>blossom</u> is the main ingredient in several soft drinks.

    (a) root   **(b)** flower   **(c)** fruit   **(d)** flesh

2. European cave <u>dwellers</u> drew pictures of mammoths with humps on their backs.

    (a) inhabitants   **(b)** immigrants   **(c)** pioneers   **(d)** skins

3. The cocoa tree bears football-shaped fruits with a <u>husk</u>.

    (a) skin   **(b)** kernel   **(c)** seed   **(d)** shoot

4. A corn <u>kernel</u> should have at least fourteen percent water so that it will pop when heated.

    (a) husk   **(b)** seed   **(c)** rind   **(d)** leaf

5. By 1830, the desire for land had drawn large numbers of <u>pioneers</u> westward.

    (a) dwellers   **(b)** settlers   **(c)** natives   **(d)** inhabitants

6. There was an old superstition that a sage plant will <u>droop</u> if its owner is ill.

    (a) peel off   **(b)** shoot up   **(c)** hang down   **(d)** dry up

7. The breadfruit is a round fruit with a rough <u>rind</u> and a soft pulpy flesh.

    (a) skin   **(b)** husk   **(c)** shell   **(d)** bloom

8. The almond, <u>native</u> to the Mediterranean, grows abundantly in California.

    (a) relative   **(b)** pioneer   **(c)** original   **(d)** immigrant

9. After the first year at Plymouth in 1620–21, half the <u>colonists</u> died.

    (a) companions   **(b)** enemies   **(c)** settlers   **(d)** foes

10. When tea leaves are picked, the <u>bud</u> and two or three leaves below are removed.

    (a) old seedling   **(b)** husk   **(c)** rind   **(d)** new leaf

PRACTICE *Vocabulary*

■■■ Chapter 6 ■■■

Words for Time and Weather

Certain adjectives and adverbs are used for specific types of description. Adverbs of time give us information about how often an event occurs. Adjectives relating to weather contrast different conditions. With a single word such as *parched*, a writer or speaker is able to paint an image that goes beyond the simple words *hot and dry*. As you read the following passage, look for adverbs of time and adjectives of weather that help make this passage vivid.

Reading Practice

The School Children's Storm

In Nebraska, the Great Blizzard of 1888 is sometimes called the "school children's storm." This is because it hit just after children had left school for the day. Many of them were caught in the storm as they walked home and never arrived.

The blizzard began on the afternoon of January 12, 1888. It came as a complete surprise. The weather that day had started out mild, so people were not dressed in their warm winter clothes. No precautions had been taken to protect livestock, and many small children were outside playing. Without warning, the wind changed direction. Snow began to fall and the temperature dropped. The snowfall was so dense that people could not see  where they were going. Many of them became lost or disoriented in the snow, and the frigid weather was responsible for many deaths.

Snowstorms, sleet, and hailstorms occur frequently in the prairie states. Blizzards are fairly common, but the Great Blizzard of 1888 is remembered as the worst of all time. To be classified as a blizzard, a winter storm must have winds of thirty-five miles per hour or more and visibility of less than one-quarter of a mile. These storm conditions must last for three hours or more.

Exercise 1

Work with a partner, with a group, or alone to answer the following questions.

1. Why weren't people prepared for the storm?

   _____

2. What was the weather like on the morning of the storm?

   _____

3. Why do Nebraskans call this blizzard "the school children's storm"?

   _____

   _____

4. What conditions must be present for a snowstorm to be called a *blizzard*?

   _____

   _____

5. How long must these conditions last?

   _____

6. Find three words to describe the weather during the blizzard.

   _____

7. Find another word for *frequent*.

   _____

8. What is the difference between *frigid* and *freezing*?

   _____

   _____

9. What types of winter weather are common in Nebraska?

   _____

   _____

■■■   PRACTICE *Vocabulary*

Conversation Practice

Read the following conversation.

Katie: Is it true you're spending the summer with your father in East Africa?

Yves: Yes, it is. My father is a photojournalist for a French television station. He travels to Africa *frequently.*

Katie: What are your travel plans?

Yves: Well, *prior to* this trip, my father has always stayed in Nairobi. He says this time we'll go straight to the Northern Frontier District. *Eventually,* we'll make our way to southwestern Kenya and Mount Kilimanjaro.

Katie: That sounds so exciting. Do you know what the weather will be like?

Yves: It's supposed to be *balmy,* since we're going at the end of the rainy season. The conditions will depend on where we are.

Katie: You mean it'll be different from place to place?

Yves: Definitely. The savannas, or plains, will be *arid* with *scorching* heat, but it should be *cool* or even *chilly* on Kilimanjaro. *Meanwhile,* on the coast at Malindi, the weather will probably be *sultry* and the air *humid.*

Katie: What's your father planning to film?

Yves: Mainly animals. They're supposed to be incredible. In the Rift Valley, where the land is flat and the grass is *parched,* there are immense herds of animals—zebras, giraffes, and gazelles. At night, you can hear the hyenas and the *occasional* roar of a lion.

Katie: You're making me envious. I wish I were going with you.

Exercise 2

Work with a partner, with a group, or alone to answer the following questions.

1. How often does Yves's father travel to Africa?

_____

2. What is an adverb that means *not very often*?

_____

3. What does *prior to* mean?

_____

4. What is the opposite of *prior to*?

_____

5. What does *eventually* mean?

_____

6. What will the weather be like, for the most part?

_____

7. Give two examples of areas where the weather is *arid*.

_____

8. Think of two places where you can find *chilly* weather.

_____

9. What is the weather like on the coast at Malindi?

_____

10. Describe the grass in the Rift Valley.

_____

Adverbs of Time

sometimes = not always; now and then

Example: Sometimes we go snowboarding when the weather isn't too cold.

occasionally = from time to time, but not regularly or often

Example: I occasionally see a famous person at the beach in Cancun.

frequently = many times; often

Example: I dive frequently during the summer.

formerly = in the past

Example: Formerly, there were no weather warnings at all.

previously = before

Example: Had you traveled to Africa previously before you made this safari?

prior to = earlier than something else

Example: No information about the weather was available prior to the storm.

eventually = at last, after a long time

Example: He eventually was able to dig his car out of the snow.

henceforth = from this time forward

Example: The governor has decided that henceforth all schools will be closed when there is a blizzard alert.

simultaneously = at the same time

Example: Is it possible to have rain and sunshine simultaneously?

meanwhile = at the same time

Example: I was making plans to travel to Asia; meanwhile, my parents were planning a trip to Africa.

Exercise 3

Circle T if the sentence is TRUE, or F if the sentence is FALSE.

1. *Formerly* means at an earlier date.   T   F

2. *Sometimes* means not during the winter.   T   F

3. *Henceforth* means from this time onward.   T   F

4. *Frequently* means often.   T   F

5. *Eventually* means at more or less the same time.   T   F

6. *Prior to* means earlier than something else.   T   F

7. *Meanwhile* means at the same time.   T   F

8. *Previously* means coming after in time or order.   T   F

9. *Occasionally* means every afternoon.   T   F

10. *Simultaneously* means at the same time.   T   F

Exercise 4

Circle the letter of the correct word or words to complete each sentence.

1. It is winter in Bogotà; _____, it is summer in Buenos Aires.

   (a) formerly   **(b)** meanwhile   **(c)** frequently

2. Ukraine was _____ part of the Soviet Union.

   (a) meanwhile   **(b)** formerly   **(c)** simultaneously

3. _____ taking a trip, your immunizations should be updated.

   (a) Prior to   **(b)** Henceforth   **(c)** Meanwhile

4. It has rained _____, so the outlook for the harvest is excellent.

   (a) frequently   **(b)** henceforth   **(c)** meanwhile

5. _____, he was a weather forecaster on television.

   (a) Previously   **(b)** Prior to   **(c)** Meanwhile

6. The town of Snowville has changed its name and will _____ be known as Blizzardville.

   (a) frequently   **(b)** henceforth   **(c)** eventually

Dry and Wet

> **arid** = having little or no moisture, usually used for areas of land
>
> > *Example:* Many areas of the southwestern United States are arid and desert-like.
>
> **parched** = excessively dry and cracked through heat or drought
>
> > *Example:* After three years of drought, the farmland was parched.
>
> **desiccated** = completely dry; without any moisture
>
> > *Example:* Using desiccated herbs when cooking is convenient.
>
> **baked** = made dry and hard by heat
>
> > *Example:* The houses were built of baked mud and bricks.
>
> **damp** = having a slight amount of moisture
>
> > *Example:* You can remove some stains with a damp cloth.
>
> **moist** = a little wet
>
> > *Example:* The roast turkey was moist and tasty.
>
> **humid** = having moisture, usually in warm air; it is often unpleasant
>
> > *Example:* Humid air is good for plants, but disagreeable for humans.
>
> **saturated** = completely filled with moisture
>
> > *Example:* His clothes were saturated after waiting in the rain for the bus.
>
> **to soak** = to make completely wet
>
> > *Example:* I soaked the seeds in water overnight before planting them.
>
> **to immerse** = to completely cover in
>
> > *Example:* To blanch vegetables, immerse them in boiling water for a few minutes.

Exercise 5

Circle T if the answer is TRUE, or F if the answer is FALSE.

1. Egyptian mummies are *desiccated*.   T   F

2. If something cracks for lack of water, it is *parched*.   T   F

3. When the air is *humid*, it is very dry.   T   F

4. *Damp* means very wet.   T   F

5. To be *immersed* is to be totally covered by liquid.   T   F

6. *Moist* is a little wet.   T   F

7. *Baked* is cooked by heat and dryness.   T   F

8. If something is *soaked*, it is completely dry.   T   F

9. A *saturated* piece of cloth can't absorb any more liquid.   T   F

10. Plants that need a lot of water do well in *arid* climates.   T   F

Exercise 6

Circle the letter of the correct word to complete each sentence.

1. After three days with no water, his lips were _____
   (a) humid.   **(b)** parched.   **(c)** saturated.

2. Camels store fat in their humps so they are able to travel in _____ lands.
   (a) arid   **(b)** soaked   **(c)** baked

3. Before the thunderstorm, the air was very _____
   (a) humid.   **(b)** soaked.   **(c)** desiccated.

4. After twenty minutes in the dryer, my socks were still _____
   (a) arid.   **(b)** immersed.   **(c)** damp.

5. She _____ the bottle to remove the label.
   (a) baked   **(b)** soaked   **(c)** parched

6. After a week of rain, the _____ ground was unable to absorb any more water.
   (a) saturated   **(b)** immersed   **(c)** moist

7. Two weeks of burning sun left the plants completely _____
   (a) humid.   **(b)** arid.   **(c)** desiccated.

8. They _____ the bread in a hot oven.
   (a) immersed   **(b)** baked   **(c)** soaked

9. She was not crying, but her eyes were _____
   (a) arid.   **(b)** moist.   **(c)** soaked.

10. To clean sheep, they are _____ in a special bath.
    (a) baked   **(b)** immersed   **(c)** parched

PRACTICE *Vocabulary*

Hot and Cold

> **scorching** = hot enough to cause damage
>
> > *Example:* The scorching heat had turned the grass brown.
>
> **sizzling** = extremely hot
>
> > *Example:* There seems to be a spell of sizzling weather every summer in the southwestern states.
>
> **sweltering** = very hot and uncomfortable
>
> > *Example:* It is very difficult to hike in the sweltering heat of the jungle.
>
> **sultry** = very hot and moist
>
> > *Example:* In the sultry days of August, everyone turns on a fan or air conditioning for relief.
>
> **stuffy** = having air that is not fresh
>
> > *Example:* Crowded with students and no open windows, the classroom was stuffy.
>
> **balmy** = soft, pleasant, and refreshing air
>
> > *Example:* We had breakfast in the garden on the balmy spring morning.
>
> **mild** = neither too hot nor too cold
>
> > *Example:* Winters are usually mild on the island because of the ocean current.
>
> **chilly** = cold enough to make one shiver a little
>
> > *Example:* The early mornings were quite chilly in the mountains.
>
> **frigid** = intense cold
>
> > *Example:* The North Pole is frigid all the time.
>
> **freezing** = very cold and icy
>
> > *Example:* The freezing temperatures in spring damaged the orange trees.

Exercise 7

Circle T if the sentence is TRUE, or F if the sentence is FALSE.

1.	*Balmy* means air that is not fresh.	T	F
2.	Wet and cold weather is *sultry*.	T	F
3.	Something *frigid* is extremely cold.	T	F
4.	Something *freezing* is extremely hot.	T	F
5.	*Scorching* means hot enough to damage.	T	F

6. *Mild* is extremely hot.   T   F

7. *Stuffy* is stale air.   T   F

8. *Sweltering* is so hot it makes you uncomfortable.   T   F

9. *Chilly* is cold enough to freeze.   T   F

10. When the weather is *sizzling*, it's unpleasantly hot.   T   F

Exercise 8

Circle the letter of the correct word to complete each sentence.

1. It was _____ in the meat freezer.

   (a) balmy   **(b)** frigid   **(c)** sizzling

2. Tropical countries generally have a _____ climate.

   (a) sultry   **(b)** freezing   **(c)** mild

3. It was too cold for my car to start in the _____ weather.

   (a) freezing   **(b)** scorching   **(c)** chilly

4. The food was so hot that it was still _____ when it reached us.

   (a) sizzling   **(b)** chilly   **(c)** sweltering

5. The temperature was _____, neither too hot nor too cold.

   (a) sweltering   **(b)** stuffy   **(c)** mild

6. With no air conditioning, it was _____ in my car.

   (a) mild   **(b)** sweltering   **(c)** frigid

7. The _____ heat from the fire melted the plastic bag.

   (a) chilly   **(b)** balmy   **(c)** scorching

8. In the evening it can be _____ enough for a jacket.

   (a) freezing   **(b)** chilly   **(c)** balmy

9. After a hot day, the evening cooled to a _____ temperature.

   (a) balmy   **(b)** stuffy   **(c)** sweltering

10. With twenty people in the small room, the air was _____

    (a) mild.   **(b)** stuffy.   **(c)** sultry.

PRACTICE *Vocabulary*

End of Chapter Test

I.

Complete each sentence with one of the following words. Write your answer on the blank line.

stuffy	prior to	saturated	sizzling	parched
damp	mild	baked	eventually	

1. Even though the semester seemed endless, we knew it would

   _____ end.

2. We were shocked to see that the land was so _____ with water; it would be impossible to plant for weeks.

3. The old house had been closed for so long that it was _____ and smelled strange.

4. After the long years of drought, the land was completely _____.

5. _____ seeing the damage caused by the storm, I had thought the reports were exaggerations.

6. Some people believe that if you go outside while your hair is

   _____, you can catch a cold.

7. The adobe bricks had _____ in the sun for several weeks.

8. We could hear the meat _____ even before we could smell it.

9. It's pleasant to take walks on _____ days when you don't even need to wear a sweater.

II.

Circle the letter of the answer that could best replace the underlined word without changing the meaning of the sentence.

1. In 1864, George Pullman designed a sleeping car that <u>eventually</u> saw widespread use.

   (a) previously
   (b) ultimately
   (c) familiarly
   (d) simultaneously

2. Freshwater turtles can survive in <u>frigid</u> waters for three months without oxygen.

   (a) balmy
   (b) sultry
   (c) freezing
   (d) sweltering

3. <u>Prior to</u> World War I, twenty percent of American homes had electricity.

   (a) Before
   (b) During
   (c) After
   (d) Despite

4. The flowering pebble is a plant that looks like a stone and grows in <u>arid</u> areas.

   (a) saturated
   (b) damp
   (c) dry
   (d) immersed

5. The <u>parched</u> landscape of salt flats is often used to break world land speed records.

   (a) dried
   (b) soaked
   (c) sultry
   (d) chilly

6. <u>Previously</u>, the economy of the United States was agrarian.

   (a) Formerly
   (b) Occasionally
   (c) Eventually
   (d) Frequently

7. Coconuts are often used in <u>desiccated</u> form in baking.

   (a) chilly
   (b) freezing
   (c) dried
   (d) baked

8. The breadfruit grows well in hot and <u>humid</u> climates.

   (a) arid
   (b) damp
   (c) soaked
   (d) desiccated

9. The water table has a level called the zone of <u>saturation</u>.

   (a) freezing
   (b) humidity
   (c) soaking
   (d) dryness

Chapter 7

Words for Locations and Occupations

You will find that it is easier to learn new words if you group them together with other words that are related. For example, think of all the words that you need to make a visit to the library. Instead of just looking up the term *check out,* find the words that have to do with the due date, the number of books you may take out, and using the various resources available in the library. You will be pleased at how quickly your vocabulary grows. In this chapter, we have selected several common locations and professions and made lists of related words for you to learn. Think about what sets of words would be useful for you to learn. Use your dictionary to make your own sets of words and then learn them.

Reading Practice

Boomer's Gym

Boomer's Gym is one of Seattle's most outstanding health clubs. It is designed to satisfy all of your health club needs. Our well-trained and friendly staff will help you choose a program to start with. You will find that exercising is a pleasure in our relaxed and comfortable atmosphere.

Our facility offers state-of-the-art equipment, expert training, dry saunas, and private lockers. Members can take classes of all levels and types, including weight training. We recommend that beginners try fitwalks, yoga, stretch classes, and muscle conditioning workouts. Intermediates can add cardio classes, kickboxing, and step interval training. At the advanced level, we offer sport conditioning, cycling, and boxing.

At Boomer's Gym, the costs are low and our customers' satisfaction is high. Visit our downtown location and you will see why our annual renewal rate is over six times the national average. If you visit us within the next thirty days, you will receive a free introductory workout, a Boomer's Gym t-shirt, and a free consultation with one of our staff members. Remember—it's never too early to start getting in shape!

Exercise 1

Work with a partner, with a group, or alone to answer the following questions.

1. What will the staff at Boomer's Gym help you do?

   _____

   _____

2. What four things does the facility offer?

   _____

   _____

3. What classes are recommended for beginners?

   _____

   _____

4. What should intermediate level club members add?

   _____

   _____

5. What is offered at the advanced level?

   _____

   _____

6. What words describe the costs and customer satisfaction at the gym?

   _____

   _____

7. How do you know that customers are satisfied?

   _____

   _____

8. What words are used to describe the gym's atmosphere?

_____

_____

9. What will you receive if you visit the gym in the next thirty days?

_____

_____

10. Where is the gym located?

_____

Conversation Practice

Read the following conversation.

Chia: Julia, what are you doing at the library so late?

Julia: I'm doing research for my term paper.

Chia: What class is it for?

Julia: World History.

Chia: Who's your teacher?

Julia: Mrs. Miller.

Chia: I had her last year, when I was a sophomore.

Julia: Did you like her?

Chia: I liked her a lot. I was sorry I couldn't take any more classes with her.

Julia: I like her, too. She's interesting and is always willing to give extra help if we need it.

Chia: So, I guess you need to get back to work. When's the paper due?

Julia: It's due tomorrow after lunch and I've still got a couple of things to check before the library closes.

Chia: Did you check resources on the Internet?

Julia: I did that already. I'm looking for a few references that I couldn't get online.

Chia: Well, good luck. I'll see you tomorrow at school.

Julia: Right. See you later.

Exercise 2

Work with a partner, with a group, or alone to answer the following questions.

1. Where is this conversation taking place?

   _____

2. What is Julia doing?

   _____

3. How does Chia know Mrs. Miller?

   _____

4. What subject does Mrs. Miller teach?

_____

5. Does Julia like Mrs. Miller? Why?

_____

_____

6. When is Julia's paper due?

_____

7. What does Julia have left to do before she can leave the library?

_____

8. Where has Julia already looked for information?

_____

9. When will Chia and Julia see each other again?

_____

10. When Julia says "See you later," does she mean later that night?

_____

Strategies

- Making lists of words related to one subject will help you remember the words. Whenever you come across a new word related to that area, add it to your list.

- Experiment with techniques for remembering the words. You may just memorize them or you may want to make cards or associations to help you remember them.

- Think about the kinds of words you need for school and daily life. Make lists of words that relate to these areas.

Situation-Specific Vocabulary

It is useful to know words connected with places, professions, school, and shopping. These are words that occur not just in specific situations, but are necessary every day. for good communication.

Example: Words from the doctor's office			
waiting room	consulting room	checkup	vaccine
shot	bandage	patient	medicine
physician	treatment	x-ray	diagnosis

Exercise 3

A. Choose three words from the box below that fit with each place listed. Write the words on the blank lines under that place. Some words in the box may not be related to either location. Work with a partner, with a group, or alone. You may use your dictionary.

language lab	salesperson	dressing room	fare
cafeteria	mirror	classroom	prescription

School

_____

_____

_____

Clothing Store

_____

_____

_____

B. Choose three words from the box below that fit with each place listed. Write the words on the blank lines under that place. Some words in the box may not be related to either location. Work with a partner, with a group, or alone. You may use your dictionary.

pump	sublet	vegetables	deli
brake fluid	registration	aisle	gasoline

Gas Station

_____

_____

_____

Supermarket

_____

_____

_____

Exercise 4

A. Choose three words from the box below that fit with each place listed. Write the words on the blank lines under that place. Some words in the box may not be related to either location. Work with a partner, with a group, or alone. You may use your dictionary.

special delivery	registered	row	usher
box office	money order	round trip	pump

Theater

_____

_____

_____

Post Office

_____

_____

_____

B. Choose three words from the box below that fit with each place listed. Write the words on the blank lines under that place. Some words in the box may not be related to either location. Work with a partner, with a group, or alone. You may use your dictionary.

jury	reference	periodicals	case
prosecutor	nonfiction	gates	departures

Courtroom   **Library**

_____   _____

_____   _____

_____   _____

Words Related to Occupations

Each occupation has its own set of vocabulary words.

***Example:** Teacher*		
midterm exam	finals	grades
research paper	assignment	lecture
course	test	tardy

Exercise 5

Match the occupations in the box with the words associated with them. Write each occupation on the correct blank line. Look up any words you don't know in your dictionary.

police officer	high school student
nurse	car salesperson
electrician	travel agent
plumber	fitness instructor
dentist	gas station attendant

1. _____

fill it up
unleaded
pump

2. _____

cavity
extraction
filling

3. _____

faucet
pipe
clog

4. _____

stretch
reach
breathe

5. _____

speeding ticket
illegal turn
driver's license

6. _____

thermometer
blood pressure
vaccine

7. _____

good mileage
test drive
monthly payment

8. _____

brochure
round trip
cruise

9. _____

freshman
locker
requirements

10. _____

fuse
wire
socket

End of Chapter Test

I.

Read the dialogues and answer the following questions. Circle the letter of the correct answer.

1. **Man:** What seems to be the problem, ma'am?
   Woman: This sink is clogged up and the faucet is dripping.

   What kind of work does the man probably do?

   (a) He's an engineer.   **(c)** He's a plumber.

   (b) He's a mechanic.   **(d)** He's an electrician.

2. **Woman:** Where can I find novels by Ernest Hemingway?
   Man: They're in aisle 3, under American Novelists.

   Where is this conversation taking place?

   (a) in a waiting room   **(c)** at a travel agency

   (b) in a bookstore   **(d)** in a supermarket

3. **Man:** Please fill it up with unleaded.
   Woman: Sure. Do you want me to check under the hood?

   What kind of work does the woman do?

   (a) She's a plumber.   **(c)** She's a gas station attendant.

   (b) She's a dentist.   **(d)** She's an engineer.

4. **Man:** I'm looking for the salad dressings.
   Woman: They're in aisle 5, next to the mustard.

   Where does this conversation take place?

   (a) in a hospital   **(c)** in a restaurant

   (b) in a clothing store   **(d)** in a supermarket

5. **Woman:** I'd like to exchange these two items.
   Man: Do you have the receipts for them?

   Where is this conversation probably taking place?

   (a) at a library   **(c)** at a bank

   (b) at a department store   **(d)** in a theater

6. **Woman:** Have you had an appointment with us before?
   Man: Yes, I came in for a flu shot last year.

   What is the woman's occupation?

   (a) She's a nurse.   **(c)** She's a dentist.

   (b) She's a teller.   **(d)** She's an engineer.

PRACTICE *Vocabulary*

7. **Man:** Will there be any breaks during this play?
   Woman: Yes, there will be a short intermission after each act.

   Where is this conversation taking place?

   (a) in a theater   (c) in a library

   (b) in a supermarket   (d) in a park

8. **Woman:** Could you have fresh towels brought to my room, please?
   Man: Certainly. I'll send someone right away.

   Where is this conversation taking place?

   (a) in a department store   (c) at a school

   (b) at a restaurant   (d) in a hotel

9. **Man:** I'd like a book of stamps, please.
   Woman: Which design would you like—the flower or the bird?
   Man: I'll take the stamps with the bird on them.

   Where is this conversation taking place?

   (a) at a drugstore   (c) at a post office

   (b) at an art gallery   (d) at the cinema

10. **Man:** Have you decided what you'd like?
    Woman: Yes, I'd like a cup of tea and a slice of peach pie, please.

    What is the man's occupation?

    (a) He's a truck driver.   (c) He's a waiter.

    (b) He's a store clerk.   (d) He's a baker.

Circle the word in each group that does not belong.

1. cotton   aspirin   beef   bandages

2. judge   gym   jury   verdict

3. ticket   schedule   brochure   witness

4. periodicals   diagnosis   fiction   reference

5. produce   meat   checkup   dairy

6. weights   deli   aerobics   instructor

7. faucet   sink   motorcycle   bathtub

8. pump   screen   aisle   usher

9. counter   menu   waiter   usher

▪▪■■ Chapter 8 ■■▪▪

Words for Thought
and Communication

This chapter introduces groups of words about thought and communication. We think in many different ways. Sometimes we *concentrate* on a single thing, and sometimes we think about very general topics. We may *meditate, contemplate,* or *reflect on* a subject. While we are thinking in all of these cases, how we go about it is subtly different. As you read the passage below, try to pick out those words and see how they convey slightly different meanings.

Reading Practice

The Loch Ness Monster

In 1933, a couple reported seeing a huge animal on the surface of Loch Ness. Since then, local residents, tourists, journalists, and scientists have tried to prove or disprove the existence of the Loch Ness Monster.

Sightings of something huge living in the lake go back to prehistoric times. When the Romans came to Scotland in the first century A.D., they found pictures of a strange beast with a long beak, a spout on its head, and flippers. In A.D. 565, Saint Columba saw a large beast in the lake about to attack a man. He saved the man by calling out God's name and ordering the beast to leave.

Since 1933 there have been thousands of sightings. Most witnesses claim to have seen a huge creature with a long neck, one or more protruding humps, and flippers. Scientists have contemplated whether such a creature exists. They have considered the possibility that the sightings are a hoax. Many of the people who claim to have seen "Nessie" are respected members of society, including teachers, scientists, and police officers.

Is there a monster? Despite the efforts of various scientific teams using sophisticated equipment, no one has produced conclusive evidence of its existence. The suggestion that Nessie is a plesiosaur, an ancient reptile that has been extinct for 65 million years, is too bizarre for most scientists to contemplate. Is it a zeuglodon, a kind of long-necked seal? Or have people been so anxious to see it that they have confused diving birds, floating plants, or mist with a sea monster?

Exercise 1

Circle T if the sentence is TRUE, or F if the sentence is FALSE.

1. The first sighting of the Loch Ness monster was in 1933.   T   F

2. Saint Columba said he saw a large beast in A.D. 565.   T   F

3. Saint Columba saw the beast about to attack a man.   T   F

4. Only tourists say they have seen the monster.   T   F

5. Scientists know there is no monster.   T   F

6. Only irresponsible people claim to have seen Nessie.   T   F

7. No conclusive evidence has been found to prove the monster's existence.   T   F

8. The plesiosaur was an ancient reptile.   T   F

9. The monster is actually a large duck.   T   F

10. People who say they saw the monster may have been confused.   T   F

Conversation Practice

Read the following conversation.

Justine: You look awfully serious today, Nick. Is something wrong?

Nick: No. I was just sitting here *reflecting* on life.

Justine: *Contemplating* your future?

Nick: How did you know?

Justine: It's a *familiar* thought for me. We'll be applying to college soon. We'll have lots of *crucial* decisions to make.

Nick: Have you decided on your major yet?

Justine: Not really. I've *speculated* on several careers. But I haven't decided on one yet. What about you?

Nick: All I know is that I don't want to do something *commonplace.* I want to do something unique, but I don't know what yet.

Justine: That's *odd.* I've been thinking the same thing. Whatever it is, I want to be well known in my field.

Nick: Of course! Nothing *petty* or *trivial* for us.

Justine: I hope not. I can't *conceive of* a boring, dull life.

PRACTICE *Vocabulary*

Exercise 2

Work with a partner, with a group, or alone to answer the following questions.

1. What is Nick doing?

   _____

2. What two thinking verbs describe what Nick is doing?

   _____

3. Is thinking about the future unusual for Justine?

   _____

4. Find another word in the conversation that is similar in meaning to *familiar*.

   _____

5. What kind of decisions will Justine and Nick have to make?

   _____

   _____

6. What kind of thing does Nick not want to do?

   _____

7. Find the word *unique* in the conversation. What is the opposite of this word?

   _____

8. What words in the conversation mean *not important*?

   _____

9. What does the word *odd* mean?

   _____

10. What is a synonym for *odd*?

   _____

Thinking and Remembering

to assume = to take as fact with no proof; to suppose

Example: I assume the Loch Ness monster is a hoax.

to reminisce = to remember or talk about the past in a pleasant way

Example: Old people often reminisce about a time when they were young.

to haunt = to be in one's thoughts, usually in an unpleasant way

Example: The scary movie he saw last week haunted his dreams.

to reflect (on) = to think over carefully

Example: He reflected on the question for a moment before he answered.

to contemplate = to think about deeply for a long time

Example: She looked at the chess board and contemplated her next move.

to meditate = to think deeply, concentrating on one matter

Example: The priest wanted to be alone and meditate before deciding.

to predict = to tell the future

Example: Weather forecasters try to predict the weather in advance.

to consider = to think about carefully in order to come to a conclusion

Example: They are considering whether to move to a new neighborhood with better schools.

to conceive (of) = to think of; to imagine

Example: It's hard to conceive of the effect that a severe earthquake can have.

to speculate = to consider something without having complete information

Example: We can only speculate about what lives at the bottom of Loch Ness.

PRACTICE *Vocabulary*

Exercise 3

Match the words in *Column A* with the definitions in *Column B*. Write the letter of the correct definition on the blank line.

Column A

_____ 1. to assume

_____ 2. to reminisce

_____ 3. to haunt

_____ 4. to reflect on

_____ 5. to contemplate

_____ 6. to meditate

_____ 7. to predict

_____ 8. to consider

_____ 9. to conceive of

_____ 10. to speculate

Column B

(a) to think about something without enough facts

(b) to think deeply, concentrating on one matter

(c) to suppose

(d) to think about carefully in order to make a decision

(e) to imagine

(f) to remember or talk about the past

(g) to think over carefully

(h) to tell beforehand

(i) to be in one's thoughts in an unpleasant way

(j) to think about deeply for a long time

Exercise 4

Circle the letter of the correct word or words to complete each sentence.

1. They refused to _____ my request to visit Loch Ness.

   (a) meditate   **(b)** reflect   **(c)** consider

2. His grandfather would often _____ about the time he was young and famous.

   (a) conceive   **(b)** predict   **(c)** reminisce

3. It is hard to _____ moving after twenty years in the same house.

   (a) contemplate   **(b)** speculate   **(c)** reminisce

4. Some athletes _____ to relax before a contest.

   (a) meditate   **(b)** predict   **(c)** conceive

5. Now that she was alone, she could _____ her past.

   (a) predict   **(b)** reflect on   **(c)** haunt

6. A billion ounces of gold is more wealth than most of us can _____

   (a) assume.   **(b)** meditate.   **(c)** conceive of.

7. He is my friend so I _____ that he is innocent.

   (a) assume   **(b)** reflect   **(c)** reminisce

8. The accident still _____ me after all this time.

   (a) considers   **(b)** haunts   **(c)** meditates

9. Some people think they can _____ the future.

   (a) predict   **(b)** reminisce   **(c)** haunt

10. We can only _____ about what the people actually saw.

    (a) predict   **(b)** reminisce   **(c)** speculate

Important and Unimportant

fundamental = basic or primary

>   *Example:* The Constitution is the fundamental law of the United States.

essential = necessary or required

>   *Example:* Oxygen is essential for us to breathe.

vital = absolutely necessary

>   *Example:* It is vital that the witness testifies in court.

indispensable = too important to be without

>   *Example:* Nurses are indispensable in a hospital.

crucial = of extreme importance; critical

>   *Example:* What we decide in the next few minutes is crucial because it will affect the rest of our lives.

drastic = sudden, extreme, and severe

>   *Example:* The government took drastic measures to control the strikes.

significant = very important

>   *Example:* Their discovery meant a significant change in the treatment of cancer.

petty = unimportant; worthless

>   *Example:* I am tired of your petty excuses for being late.

trivial = having little value or importance

>   *Example:* She worries about trivial things, like what's on TV, instead of important ones like finding a job.

mere = nothing more than; only

>   *Example:* What do you expect? He's a mere child.

Exercise 5

Circle T if the sentence is TRUE, or F if the sentence is FALSE.

1. *Drastic* means something important.   T   F

2. Something *vital* is absolutely necessary.   T   F

3. Something *trivial* is not important.   T   F

4. Something basic is *fundamental*.   T   F

5. *Mere* means something is more than it appears.   T   F

6. Something *essential* cannot be removed without destroying   T   F
   the whole.

7. *Indispensable* means you can throw it away.   T   F

8. Something *petty* is very important.   T   F

9. *Crucial* can describe an important decision.   T   F

10. Something *significant* is very important.   T   F

Exercise 6

Circle the letter of the correct word to complete each sentence.

1. The computer was _____ to our project—without it, we couldn't have finished.

   (a) indispensable   (b) drastic   (c) significant

2. A tornado requires _____ action by people in its path.

   (a) mere   (b) petty   (c) drastic

3. The _____ goal of this class is to improve vocabulary skills.

   (a) fundamental   (b) vital   (c) significant

4. It is silly to get upset over _____ mistakes.

   (a) essential   (b) trivial   (c) drastic

5. To take the exam now or to wait a year is a _____ decision.

   (a) drastic   (b) mere   (c) crucial

6. His speech was _____ to all those in the audience who would lose their jobs in
   the layoffs.

   (a) fundamental   (b) petty   (c) significant

7. Their latest threat is a _____ scare tactic.

   (a) mere   (b) essential   (c) fundamental

PRACTICE *Vocabulary*

8. A/An _____ part of being a hero is not thinking before you take action.

   (a) trivial   **(b)** petty   **(c)** essential

9. When there are so many important things to be done, why does she insist on so many _____ details?

   (a) drastic   **(b)** petty   **(c)** vital

10. It is _____ that you get this message to John, or we won't be able to finish the project.

   (a) vital   **(b)** indispensable   **(c)** mere

Usual and Unusual

familiar = similar to what one already knows

> *Example:* When he talked about his problems, they were familiar to us.

commonplace = found everywhere; not special

> *Example:* Car thefts are commonplace in this city.

unique = the only one of its kind

> *Example:* Each person's fingerprints are unique.

singular = different or strange

> *Example:* After I had caught the snake, I experienced a singular feeling I can't describe.

prevalent = widely existing

> *Example:* Malaria is prevalent in hot, swampy areas.

widespread = found or occurring in many places

> *Example:* Hoof and mouth disease is widespread because it is so hard to control.

odd = not usual; strange

> *Example:* I don't know what job he has, but he leaves at odd hours.

peculiar = out of the ordinary; strange

> *Example:* This sauce has a very peculiar taste.

eccentric = not following usual rules of behavior

> *Example:* His teacher had the eccentric habit of cutting his fingernails in class.

scarce = not common; hard to find

> *Example:* Environmental conditions have made certain birds scarce.

Exercise 7

Circle T if the sentence is TRUE, or F if the sentence is FALSE.

1. Something that is *odd* is not commonplace.   T   F

2. An *eccentric* habit is an unusual one.   T   F

3. If a thing is *widespread*, it is hard to find.   T   F

4. Something *scarce* is frightening.   T   F

5. Things that are *commonplace* can be found everywhere.   T   F

6. *Singular* means usual and like everything else.   T   F

7. Something *peculiar* has a strange aspect.   T   F

8. A *unique* object has no equal.   T   F

9. If something is *prevalent*, it is scarce.   T   F

10. Almost everybody recognizes a *familiar* face.   T   F

Exercise 8

Circle the letter of the correct word to complete each sentence.

1. The price of fruit increased because it was _____

   (a) prevalent.   **(b)** odd.   **(c)** scarce.

2. His purple hair and brightly-colored clothes gave him a _____ appearance.

   (a) singular   **(b)** scarce   **(c)** widespread

3. Diseases are _____ in many countries.

   (a) prevalent   **(b)** eccentric   **(c)** peculiar

4. The man frightened me with his _____ smile.

   (a) familiar   **(b)** scarce   **(c)** peculiar

5. The handmade car sold for a million dollars because it was _____

   (a) unique.   **(b)** scarce.   **(c)** commonplace.

6. The _____ old woman wore a winter coat in hot weather.

   (a) familiar   **(b)** eccentric   **(c)** commonplace

End of Chapter Test

Circle the letter of the answer that could best replace the underlined word or words without changing the meaning of the sentence.

1. <u>Reflecting on</u> your problems won't help you solve them.

   (a) Thinking about   **(c)** Predicting

   (b) Repeating   **(d)** Talking about

2. The Loch Ness monster is a <u>unique</u> creature.

   (a) commonplace   **(c)** singular

   (b) scarce   **(d)** prevalent

3. Plenty of rest is <u>indispensable</u> before a marathon.

   (a) commonplace   **(c)** necessary

   (b) trivial   **(d)** significant

4. I guess I just <u>assumed</u> that the experiment would prove the theory.

   (a) supposed   **(c)** haunted

   (b) conceived   **(d)** suspected

5. I don't think such <u>drastic</u> measures were called for.

   (a) trivial   **(c)** petty

   (b) extreme   **(d)** essential

6. It is hard to <u>conceive of</u> a situation that would require calling the police.

   (a) produce   **(c)** predict

   (b) meditate   **(d)** imagine

7. No one thinks his or her own problems are <u>trivial</u>.

   (a) significant   **(c)** unimportant

   (b) drastic   **(d)** severe

8. Someday we will probably <u>reminisce</u> about high school.

   (a) forget   **(c)** remember

   (b) predict   **(d)** speculate

9. What seems <u>strange</u> to one person may seem normal to another.

   (a) mere   **(c)** odd

   (b) fundamental   **(d)** petty

10. Before you pick a college, you should <u>consider</u> many factors.

    (a) meditate   **(c)** remember

    (b) think carefully about   **(d)** speculate

Chapter 8: *Words for Thought and Communication*   ▪▪▪ 111

■■■ Chapter 9 ■■■

Words for
Feelings and Sensations

Native speakers know that when they speak about feelings and sensations, they can choose to use words that describe different degrees or extremes of them. The words *mean* and *ruthless* both refer to unkindness, but they have very different meanings. Someone who is *mean* is not kind. Someone who is *ruthless* is so mean that he or she shows no pity or kindness at all. The same is true with words that describe taste sensations. They range from *tasteless,* having no taste at all, to *pungent,* which may have so much taste it is inedible. In this chapter you will learn some of the words you need to describe feelings and sensations more accurately.

Reading Practice

Ageusia

Did you know that there is such a thing as a taste disorder? Some people are unable to taste at all. This disorder is called *ageusia.* It is not very common, because the brain receives information about taste from three different nerves. Nevertheless, about 2 million North Americans suffer from this condition.

Imagine not being able to taste. You would not be able to tell the difference between food that was pungent or insipid, spicy or bland. Actually, there are really only four basic tastes. They are sweet, salty, sour, and bitter. Everything else we taste is a combination of these four tastes. A fifth taste, *umani,* has recently been identified. It is a taste that occurs only when foods with *glutamate* are eaten.

Taste buds are found on the tongue. There are also special taste receptor cells on the palate (the roof of the mouth) and at the entrance to the pharynx. These all are receptors of taste. Different parts of the tongue are sensitive to specific tastes. The tip of the tongue tastes sweetness, the back bitterness, the sides sourness and saltiness. The more taste buds we have, the more sensitive our tongues are to these tastes. Taste buds only live a short time and then are replaced. As we get older, our sense of taste becomes diminished. This may be because taste buds are not replaced as quickly as they were when we were young.

Exercise 1

Work with a partner, with a group, or alone to answer the following questions.

1. What is the name of the disorder that makes people unable to taste?

_____

2. Are taste disorders common? Why or why not?

_____

3. List the four basic types of taste that are mentioned in the passage.

_____

4. What are the actual receptors of taste?

_____

5. What is the name of the new taste recently discovered?

_____

6. What has to be eaten for us to taste *umani?*

_____

7. Where do we taste sweetness?

_____

8. Where do we taste bitterness?

_____

9. What determines how sensitive to taste our tongues are?

_____

10. What is a possible reason for why older people taste less?

_____

PRACTICE *Vocabulary*

Conversation Practice

Read the following conversation.

Maria: Excuse me. Is this the right way to get to Eagle Lake?

Kien: Yes, it's less than a mile to the Eagle Crest. From there, it's about one-half mile to the lake.

Maria: That's a relief. I was beginning to think I was lost.

Kien: I thought you were looking a little ***apprehensive***. My group is hiking to the lake, too. Would you like to come with us?

Maria: Thanks. That's really ***considerate*** of you. I guess I'm not as ***bold*** as I thought I would be.

Kien: Well, you know it's not a good idea to hike alone on this mountain. No matter how ***courageous*** you are, it's best to hike with one or more people.

Maria: Yes, it was foolish of me, I know. I won't do it again.

Kien: Why don't you sit down on this log for a minute and rest until my friends catch up? How about some lemonade? It's a little sour but it's cold.

Maria: Thank you. That would be great. You're very ***generous***. I was lucky to run into you today.

Kien: Oh, here's my group. Are you ready to go on?

Maria: Ready!

Exercise 2

Work with a partner, with a group, or alone to answer the following questions.

1. How did Kien think Maria looked?

   _____

2. Why did she look that way?

   _____

3. What does Maria think about Kien when he invites her to hike with his group?

   _____

4. What does Maria think about herself?

   _____

5. What kind of taste does the lemonade have?

   _____

6. What does Maria think about Kien after he offers her some lemonade?

   _____

7. What do you call a person who doesn't share anything?

   _____

8. Was it brave of Maria to try to climb the mountain alone?

   _____

9. What does Kien think about climbing alone?

   _____

10. Will Maria hike on this mountain alone again?

   _____

PRACTICE *Vocabulary*

Kindness and Unkindness

benevolent = doing good deeds; kindly

> *Example:* Michael Faraday was so benevolent that he gave away all of the money he earned from his inventions.

benign = good-natured; harmless

> *Example:* He was in a benign mood after visiting his favorite aunt.

humane = showing kindness and compassion

> *Example:* It was humane of them to stop and help the injured dog.

considerate = thoughtful of others; concerned with others' feelings

> *Example:* It was very considerate of her to come and take care of me when I was sick.

generous = willing to give or share

> *Example:* She was generous with her time in volunteering for the animal shelter.

selfish = wanting everything for oneself

> *Example:* Selfish people need to learn how to share with others.

mean = unkind; disagreeable

> *Example:* He has a mean-looking face, but he's actually quite kind.

spiteful = annoying or hurtful on purpose

> *Example:* The girl destroyed her sister's doll just to be spiteful.

merciless = cruel; having no kindness

> *Example:* The enemy was merciless and drove all the people from their homes.

ruthless = having no compassion or kindness

> *Example:* Everyone knew the commander was a ruthless person who would do anything to gain power.

Exercise 3

Circle T if the sentence is TRUE, or F if the sentence is FALSE.

1. Someone who is *selfish* wants everything for himself or herself.   T   F

2. A *merciless* person is not cruel.   T   F

3. To be *benign* is to be good-natured.   T   F

4. A *generous* person takes everything he or she can get.   T   F

5. *Ruthless* means unable to be cruel.   T   F

6. A *mean* person is kind and generous.   T   F

7. A *benevolent* person wants to do good and be kind.   T   F

8. *Spiteful* behavior is kind and gentle.   T   F

9. A *humane* person is cruel and selfish.   T   F

10. Being *considerate* means being thoughtful of others.   T   F

Exercise 4

Circle the letter of the correct word to complete each sentence.

1. They say that people who treat animals in a _____ way are kind to people, too.

   (a) selfish   (b) merciless   (c) humane

2. A _____ businessman is one who destroys his competitors.

   (a) considerate   (b) benevolent   (c) ruthless

3. A _____ person hurts you in little ways.

   (a) spiteful   (b) merciless   (c) benign

4. The king was a good man and a _____ leader of his people.

   (a) selfish   (b) merciless   (c) benign

5. She was a _____ enemy and never gave her opponent even the smallest chance.

   (a) merciless   (b) spiteful   (c) selfish

6. A _____ man, he always gave money to the poor.

   (a) ruthless   (b) selfish   (c) generous

7. She was so _____ of others that she was liked by everyone.

   (a) mean   (b) considerate   (c) merciless

8. He is so _____ he won't even give you one french fry!

   (a) benign   (b) generous   (c) selfish

9. The _____ woman made a point of visiting people in the hospital who had no relatives to visit them.

   (a) benevolent   (b) mean   (c) ruthless

10. It is _____ to tie your grandmother's shoelaces together.

   (a) considerate   (b) mean   (c) selfish

Fear and Courage

---

scared = afraid; frightened

    Example: With all those strange noises, I was scared in that house at night.

timid = not having courage

    Example: Some students are too timid to speak in class.

apprehensive = anxious about the future

    Example: In the 1940s, people were right to be apprehensive of war.

cowardly = unable to face danger because of a lack of courage

    Example: His cowardly behavior made everyone avoid him.

petrified = unable to move because of fear

    Example: People were petrified when they saw the tidal wave approaching.

bold = willing to face danger

    Example: She was bold to volunteer to cross enemy lines.

courageous = having no fear; being brave

    Example: During the blizzard, some courageous people risked their own lives to help save others.

daring = willing to take risks; without fear

    Example: It was daring of her to climb that mountain.

intrepid = not afraid; very brave

    Example: The couple, intrepid explorers, went into the Amazon.

audacious = extremely daring

    Example: Walking up to the president of that company and asking for a job was audacious of you.

Exercise 5

Circle T if the sentence is TRUE, or F if the sentence is FALSE.

1. *Daring* means not taking risks.   T   F

2. If you are too afraid to move, you are *petrified*.   T   F

3. *Timid* means not having the time to be afraid.   T   F

4. If you are *bold*, you are willing to face danger.   T   F

5. *Apprehensive* is being afraid about the future.   T   F

6. A *cowardly* person runs toward danger.   T   F

7. *Audacious* means extremely daring.   T   F

8. A *courageous* person does brave things.   T   F

9. A *scared* person is afraid.   T   F

10. *Intrepid* means ready to run away.   T   F

Exercise 6

Circle the letter of the correct word to complete each sentence.

1. It was a _____ move to say no to the boss.
   (a) cowardly   **(b)** timid   **(c)** bold

2. To swim across the river at night was _____ of him.
   (a) audacious   **(b)** scared   **(c)** timid

3. It was _____ of her to pull the children from the fire.
   (a) cowardly   **(b)** courageous   **(c)** apprehensive

4. It was _____ of her to run and hide.
   (a) intrepid   **(b)** cowardly   **(c)** audacious

5. When she rode a bicycle for the first time, she was a little bit _____
   (a) intrepid.   **(b)** petrified.   **(c)** scared.

6. Many people are _____ about flying.
   (a) apprehensive   **(b)** audacious   **(c)** cowardly

7. If you are _____ in business, you will not succeed.
   (a) intrepid   **(b)** timid   **(c)** bold

8. It will take a very _____ plan to surprise them.
   (a) apprehensive   **(b)** scared   **(c)** daring

9. The _____ hiker could not be discouraged from climbing every peak.

    (a) intrepid   **(b)** apprehensive   **(c)** petrified

10. When the captain announced there was engine trouble with our airplane, we were all _____

    (a) intrepid.   **(b)** daring.   **(c)** petrified.

Types of Taste

tasteless = having no flavor at all

    Example: People say this fruit is delicious, but I find it tasteless.

bland = without much taste; very mild

    Example: Boiled potatoes with nothing on them seem bland to many people.

insipid = having a very weak flavor

    Example: All the food they served me in the hospital was insipid.

flavorful = tasty

    Example: The children enjoy chocolate milk because it is so flavorful.

savory = having a pleasant taste that is not sweet

    Example: Some people prefer savory desserts like cheese and crackers to sweet ones.

sour = having a taste that is not sweet, such as vinegar or lemons

    Example: These grapes are too sour to eat.

bitter = having a sharp taste that is not sweet or sour, as in some medicines

    Example: When tea is too strong, it can taste bitter.

spicy = containing seasonings like pepper or ginger

    Example: Spicy tofu with peppers is my favorite dish.

pungent = having a strong or sharp taste or smell

    Example: That pungent smell made my dog sneeze.

hot = very spicy

    Example: You put so much chili in the stew that it's too hot to eat.

Exercise 7

Circle T if the sentence is TRUE, or F if the sentence is FALSE.

1. *Spicy* means too cold to taste.   T   F

2. Something *flavored* is tasteless.   T   F

3. *Hot* means very spicy.   T   F

4. Something *bitter* has no sweetness or sourness and is sharp to taste.   T   F

5. *Bland* food has a very strong flavor.   T   F

6. Something *pungent* has a strong, sharp taste or smell.   T   F

7. *Savory* means having a pleasant taste that is not sweet.   T   F

8. Something *insipid* has a very weak flavor.   T   F

9. A lemon usually has a very *sour* taste.   T   F

10. *Tasteless* food is too spicy for some people to eat.   T   F

Exercise 8

Circle the letter of the correct word to complete each sentence.

1. The strong garlic sauce had a _____ flavor.
    (a) sour   (b) bland   (c) pungent

2. Many types of sausage are made _____ by adding pepper.
    (a) hot   (b) bitter   (c) bland

3. The guests enjoyed _____ snacks at the reception.
    (a) savory   (b) insipid   (c) tasteless

4. Without sugar or raisins, oatmeal tastes very _____
    (a) spicy.   (b) flavored.   (c) bland.

5. Yogurt has a naturally _____ taste.
    (a) savory   (b) sour   (c) pungent

6. Strong coffee is _____
    (a) bitter.   (b) spicy.   (c) bland.

7. Do you like duck _____ with orange?
    (a) bitter   (b) bland   (c) flavored

8. I like _____ food, but it makes me feel ill after I eat it.
    (a) spicy   (b) insipid   (c) bland

9. The soup was so plain it tasted _____
    (a) spicy.   (b) insipid.   (c) hot.

10. Clean water should be _____
    (a) insipid.   (b) sour.   (c) tasteless.

PRACTICE *Vocabulary*

End of Chapter Test

I.

Complete each sentence with one of the following words. Use each word only once. Write the word on the blank line.

pungent	flavored	bitter	merciless	cowardly
mean	spiteful	petrified	intrepid	apprehensive

1. The cough syrup was so _____, the baby refused to swallow it.

2. Everyone thought the teacher was _____, until she offered to help students after school and on weekends.

3. It isn't _____ to refuse to take unnecessary risks.

4. The whole room was filled with the _____ smell of the spices.

5. Her frequent insults were _____ and immature.

6. The _____ archaeologist discovered a new temple in the Guatemalan jungle.

7. I didn't like the strawberry _____ toothpaste.

8. I was a little bit _____ about going directly into an intermediate level class.

9. His _____ teasing finally made his sister so angry she screamed.

10. When the door suddenly slammed shut behind us, we were too

_____ to move.

II.

Circle the letter of the answer that could best replace the underlined word without changing the meaning of the sentence.

1. Bats are surprisingly <u>timid</u> creatures.

    (a) shy **(b)** audacious **(c)** petrified **(d)** considerable

2. Paul Revere <u>daringly</u> rode through the New England countryside to warn the colonists.

    (a) benevolently **(b)** courageously **(c)** apprehensively **(d)** mercilessly

3. A <u>benign</u> lesion usually has a regular border.

    (a) humane **(b)** petrified **(c)** congenial **(d)** harmless

4. Acorns are <u>bitter</u> to taste.

    (a) sharp **(b)** sour **(c)** bland **(d)** intrepid

5. Robert Peary, an <u>intrepid</u> explorer, was the first to reach the North Pole.

    (a) daring **(b)** ruthless **(c)** spiteful **(d)** insipid

6. The <u>benevolent</u> Emma Willard started women's education by opening a school in her home in 1814.

    (a) apprehensive **(b)** merciless **(c)** spiteful **(d)** kind

7. It took a great deal of <u>courage</u> for the early explorers to set sail on uncharted seas.

    (a) foolishness **(b)** bravery **(c)** benevolence **(d)** timidity

8. Many of America's parks have been made possible through <u>generous</u> private donations.

    (a) kindhearted **(b)** ruthless **(c)** selfish **(d)** audacious

9. Eating <u>flavored</u> ices is a delicious way to cool off in the summer.

    (a) bland **(b)** bitter **(c)** pungent **(d)** special-tasting

10. She received recognition for her <u>humane</u> treatment of the city's poorest citizens.

    (a) bitter **(b)** merciless **(c)** ruthless **(d)** kind

PRACTICE *Vocabulary*

■■■ Chapter 10 ■■■

Words for Size

You may be surprised at how many different ways there are to describe dimensions and proportions in English. From *gigantic* to *microscopic*, we can group words by the conditions they describe, *big* and *small, getting bigger* and *getting smaller.* Objects can *shrink* until they seem to disappear, or *swell* until they burst. You may find these words in your science and math books. Try to find all the words that describe size as you read about the Micromouse below.

Reading Practice

The Micromouse

The Micromouse is a diminutive computer that is designed to find its way through a maze. It is an electromechanical device that is self-contained. This means the entire control system is within the mouse itself. The maximum length and width of a Micromouse is 25 cm x 25 cm. This is because it must be able to move through the miniature maze. The Micromouse may be as tall as its designers decide to build it.

Micromice compete in contests to see which of the miniscule computers can achieve the fastest time running through an unknown maze. Usually the mouse has to make several runs through the maze before it can gain speed. Each time it goes through the maze, it gathers and stores information about the maze. This information allows it to calculate the fastest path. A contestant may not take more than fifteen minutes per run.

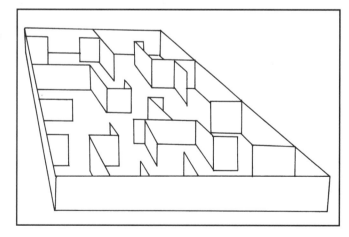

Micromice are often built by teams. A typical team may include mechanical engineers, electrical engineers, computer scientists, and physicists. They put a great deal of time and effort into developing the tiny contestants. Competitions are held at a number of universities throughout the year.

Exercise 1

Work with a partner, with a group, or alone to answer these questions. You may use your dictionary.

1. What is a Micromouse?

   _____

2. Find four words that mean *small*.

   _____

   _____

3. What is the maximum height of a Micromouse?

   _____

4. Why are the width and length of the Micromouse limited?

   _____

5. What is a *maze*?

   _____

6. What does *self-contained* mean?

   _____

7. What must the Micromouse do to win?

   _____

8. Why is the first run through the maze the slowest?

   _____

9. Name four types of professionals who might work on a Micromouse.

   _____

   _____

10. Where do most Micromouse competitions take place?

   _____

Conversation Practice

Read the following conversation.

Alec: Hi! I tried to call you yesterday. Where were you?

Nadia: I went to the Natural History Museum to see the *expanded* dinosaur exhibit.

Alec: Did you like it?

Nadia: A lot. It was amazing to see how big most of the dinosaurs were. The full-sized models *dwarf* everything else at the museum.

Alec: I'll have to go see it for myself. Maybe I'll get some information for my biology term paper. I want to write about the theories concerning the *decline* and *extinction* of the dinosaurs.

Nadia: Well, there's lots of information at the museum that could *augment* your library and Internet research.

Alec: Good. Then I'll definitely go on Saturday.

Nadia: Let me know how you like it.

Alec: I will. See you after class.

Exercise 2

Work with a partner, with a group, or alone to answer the following questions.

1. What did Nadia go to see at the Natural History Museum?

   _____

2. What does Nadia mean by an *expanded* exhibit?

   _____

3. What do the full-sized models do in relation to the other things at the museum?

   _____

4. What does Alec want to write about for his biology term paper?

   _____

5. What does *decline* mean?

   _____

6. What does *extinction* mean?

   _____

7. How could visiting the museum help Alec with his term paper?

   _____

   _____

8. What does *augment* mean?

   _____

9. What does a *dwarf* plant look like?

   _____

10. Name three places where Alec can find information for his paper.

   _____

   _____

Growing and Getting Bigger

to expand = to grow larger

> *Example:* A dry sponge expands when soaked in water.

to amplify = to make greater or stronger, especially used for sound

> *Example:* There are several kinds of devices that can be used to amplify a speaker's voice.

to augment = to add to; to enlarge

> *Example:* The victory augmented his confidence even more.

to boom = to grow rapidly

> *Example:* The housing market was booming last year.

to boost = to increase in amount

> *Example:* Free samples were given with every purchase to boost sales of the new product.

to prosper = to continue to succeed in life, health, and wealth

> *Example:* There was no other store like it in the village, so it prospered.

to flourish = to grow with strength

> *Example:* The plants in the garden flourished under her care.

to swell = to expand or get larger because of internal pressure

> *Example:* When he broke his finger, it started to swell.

to prolong = to make longer in time

> *Example:* He prolonged his stay by an extra two days.

Exercise 3

Circle T if the sentence is TRUE, or F if the sentence is FALSE.

1. To *boom* is to grow quickly.   T   F

2. To *boost* is to kick hard.   T   F

3. To be successful and continue in that way is to *prosper*.   T   F

4. To *augment* is to give away.   T   F

5. To grow with strength is to *flourish*.   T   F

6. To increase the strength of something is to *amplify*.   T   F

7. To make longer in time is to *prolong*.   T   F

8. To *expand* is to cost more.   T   F

9. To *swell* is to expand because of pressure.   T   F

Exercise 4

Complete each sentence with one of the following words. Change the verb form if necessary. Write the word on the blank line.

expand	amplify	augment	swell	boom
boost	prosper	flourish	prolong	

1. He _____ the music so that it could be heard outside.

2. Thanks to much hard work and a little luck, his company

   _____ .

3. It was so nice by the ocean that they _____ their stay.

4. With love and a healthy diet, the children _____ .

5. When he breathes in, his chest _____ by six inches.

6. The latest victory _____ their chances of winning the series.

7. The computer industry has _____ over the last two decades.

8. Getting a good grade _____ your confidence.

9. The rotten fruit _____ until it burst.

Big

---

large = bigger than usual

  Example: I was surprised to see how large their house is.

great = large or important

  Example: Walking on the moon was a great achievement.

grand = important and large in degree

  Example: All of the grand plans she had made fell through when she lost
    her job.

huge = very large in size or amount

  Example: A huge crowd had formed in front of the embassy.

massive = extremely large in size, amount, or number

  Example: A massive landslide blocked the main road to town for three days.

immense = extremely large in size or degree

  Example: An immense amount of money is wasted on junk food.

enormous = extremely large

  Example: I ate an enormous slice of melon for breakfast this morning.

gigantic = extremely large

  Example: There is a gigantic hole in the ozone layer.

colossal = of great size; huge

  Example: The pyramids in Egypt are colossal structures.

Exercise 5

Circle T if the sentence is TRUE, or F if the sentence is false.

1. An *immense* building is extremely large.   T   F

2. If you have a *huge* amount of work, you are extremely busy.   T   F

3. Someone with an *enormous* appetite is never hungry.   T   F

4. A *gigantic* spider is smaller than a large one.   T   F

5. If your party was a *grand* affair, it was small and casual.   T   F

6. A *massive* oil spill can do *immense* harm to the environment.   T   F

7. The Great Wall of China is a *colossal* structure.   T   F

8. If you waste a *great* amount of time on your homework, you may not finish it.   T   F

Exercise 6

Circle the letter of the correct word to complete each sentence.

1. It was a _____ mistake to drive from San Francisco to San Diego in one day.

   (a) huge   **(b)** hugest   **(c)** long

2. The results of our experiment were wrong because of a/an _____ error in our calculations.

   (a) bigger   **(b)** immense   **(c)** considerate

3. The _____ your ambitions, the more likely you will be to succeed.

   (a) immenser   **(b)** huger   **(c)** greater

4. A whale shark appears as a _____ shadow under water.

   (a) grandest   **(b)** gigantic   **(c)** flourish

5. The most _____ collection of insects I have ever seen came from the Brazilian rain forests.

   (a) enormous   **(b)** enormouser   **(c)** enormousest

6. Our honeymoon was a _____ vacation.

   (a) gigantic   **(b)** massive   **(c)** grand

7. A _____ power shortage led to cuts in the electrical service.

   (a) massive   **(b)** bigger   **(c)** hugest

8. The first computers were so _____ they often filled a room.

   (a) augmented   **(b)** grandest   **(c)** gigantic

Getting Smaller

to shrink = to become smaller in size

Example: Wool often shrinks when it is washed in hot water.

to decline = to lessen in force, power, or value

Example: His power began to decline after he lost a succession of battles.

to diminish = to make smaller or lesser

Example: His popularity diminished after he was caught cheating on the test.

to condense = to reduce in volume

Example: The four-page article was condensed into a paragraph.

to contract = to become smaller by drawing together

Example: The heart circulates blood by contracting and expanding.

to subside = to become less active or intense

Example: Before starting on their trip, they waited for the winds to subside.

to abate = to reduce in force, degree, or strength

Example: The strong pains in his stomach showed no signs of abating.

to decrease = to become less in number, strength, or quality

Example: When mixed with water, the strength of the solution will decrease.

to reduce = to lessen in any way

Example: We reduced our prices so that we could sell more computers.

to dwindle = to become smaller or less

Example: We saw the flames dwindle and finally disappear.

Exercise 7

Circle T if the sentence is TRUE, or F if the sentence is FALSE.

1. When something strong becomes weak, it *abates*.   T   F

2. To *reduce* is to lessen in any way.   T   F

3. If something becomes less active or intense, it *subsides*.   T   F

4. To *condense* is to reduce in volume.   T   F

5. If you *decrease* something, you make it flatter.   T   F

6. Something that *declines* lessens in value, power, or force.   T   F

7. To *diminish* is to become cheaper.   T   F

8. To *dwindle* is to become smaller or less.   T   F

9. To *shrink* is to fall from a high point.   T   F

10. To *contract* is to become smaller by drawing together.   T   F

Exercise 8

Circle the letter of the correct word to complete each sentence.

1. After five hours, the storm _____

   (a) contracted.   **(b)** abated.   **(c)** shrank.

2. The pupils of your eyes _____ in bright light.

   (a) contract   **(b)** diminish   **(c)** dwindle

3. Ten minutes after winning the lottery, his joy _____

   (a) subsided.   **(b)** condensed.   **(c)** reduced.

4. Hikers can buy _____ milk, which is easier to carry.

   (a) abated   **(b)** dwindled   **(c)** condensed

5. After changing their product, sales _____

   (a) diminished.   **(b)** condensed.   **(c)** contracted.

6. The number of cigarette smokers has _____ in the United States.

   (a) subsided   **(b)** condensed   **(c)** decreased

7. When you cook meat, it _____

   (a) dwindles.   **(b)** abates.   **(c)** shrinks.

8. We _____ our water bills by washing the car only once a week.

   (a) reduced   **(b)** subsided   **(c)** condensed

9. The planet's resources are _____ as the years go by.

   (a) condensing   **(b)** abating   **(c)** dwindling

10. Natural disasters can cause the greatest nations to _____

   (a) decrease.   **(b)** decline.   **(c)** reduce.

Small

---

tiny = very small

> *Example:* A newborn baby has tiny hands and feet.

minute = very small

> *Example:* All the information you need is stored in a minute chip in the computer.

diminutive = very small

> *Example:* As technology has progressed, more diminutive versions of the pocket calculator have been developed.

to dwarf = to make something look small by comparison

> *Example:* That full-grown oak tree dwarfs the seedling I just planted.

minuscule = very, very small

> *Example:* The minuscule print was almost impossible to read.

minimal = the smallest possible amount or degree

> *Example:* The injuries he suffered from the accident were minimal.

miniature = a very small copy or example of something

> *Example:* Miniature portraits the size of a coin were popular at one time.

microscopic = so small it can only be seen with a microscope

> *Example:* Though microscopic in size, the flu virus can have fatal effects on the elderly.

Exercise 9

Circle T if the sentence is TRUE, or F if the sentence is FALSE.

1. A dinosaur is *minute*.   T   F

2. Something *minimal* comes in small sizes.   T   F

3. *Tiny* means very small.   T   F

4. To *dwarf* something means to make it look large.   T   F

5. The Statue of Liberty is *diminutive*.   T   F

6. Something *minuscule* takes up a lot of room.   T   F

7. *Microscopic* things cannot be seen without microscopes.   T   F

8. Something *miniature* is smaller than natural size.   T   F

Exercise 10

Circle the letter of the correct word to complete each sentence.

1. John _____ me because he is so tall.

    (a) dwarfs   **(b)** microscopic   **(c)** minimal

2. Sybil and Jerry's new puppy is really _____

    (a) tiny.   **(b)** minimal.   **(c)** miniature.

3. The detectives took the victim's clothes for a _____ examination.

    (a) microscopic   **(b)** miniature   **(c)** miniscule

4. With _____ effort, she won the downhill ski event.

    (a) minimal   **(b)** diminutive   **(c)** microscopic

5. She may be a _____ woman, but she still likes to play basketball.

    (a) microscopic   **(b)** minuscule   **(c)** diminutive

6. The restaurant was expensive and the steaks were _____

    (a) microscopic.   **(b)** dwarf.   **(c)** minuscule.

7. She had a seventeenth-century _____ portrait of a distant relative.

    (a) minute   **(b)** miniature   **(c)** minimal

8. Who would win the race depended on a _____ time difference.

    (a) minute   **(b)** miniature   **(c)** diminutive

PRACTICE *Vocabulary*

End of Chapter Test

I.

Complete each sentence with one of the following words. Change the verb form if necessary. Write the word on the blank line.

swell	minimal	miniature	diminutive	boost
dwindle	augment	microscopic	prolong	condensed

1. With a _____ amount of effort, you could pass this course.

2. We could _____ our sales by advertising in the Sunday paper.

3. As the semester progressed, the students' interest _____.

4. If you put a sponge in water, it will _____.

5. Dust mites are _____ creatures that live in mattresses and pillows.

6. The _____ hummingbird is able to suspend itself in the air and fly backward.

7. We _____ production by using fertilizer.

8. It's easy to prepare _____ soup by adding water and heating it.

9. A _____ dog can live in an apartment.

10. The test was postponed till the next week, _____ the students' suffering.

II.

Circle the letter of the answer that could best replace the underlined word without changing the meaning of the sentence.

1. A lie detector detects <u>minute</u> changes in a person's breathing rate and pulse.

   (a) dormant   **(b)** momentary   **(c)** dwarf   **(d)** tiny

2. The plant life in tundra regions includes mosses, <u>dwarf</u> shrubs, and some flowers.

   (a) microscopic   **(b)** minuscule   **(c)** flourishing   **(d)** diminutive

3. The jute plant, a relative of the basswood tree, <u>flourishes</u> in warm, humid climates.

   (a) amplifies   **(b)** swells   **(c)** thrives   **(d)** prolongs

4. Originally developed for southern California, the use of the Richter scale has been <u>expanded</u> to include the rest of the world.

   (a) prolonged   **(b)** enlarged   **(c)** minuscule   **(d)** amplified

5. The underwater telegraph cable has a number of relay stations to <u>boost</u> the signal.

   (a) strengthen   **(b)** prosper   **(c)** swell   **(d)** subside

6. Viruses are <u>microscopic</u> organisms that cause a number of diseases in people, animals, and even plants.

   (a) extremely minute   **(b)** very active   **(c)** out of proportion   **(d)** enlarged

7. Many California mining towns <u>prospered</u> until the gold mines ran dry.

   (a) declined   **(b)** assembled   **(c)** employed   **(d)** thrived

8. Dieting can <u>decrease</u> your weight.

   (a) boom   **(b)** diminish   **(c)** abate   **(d)** expand

9. Supplies of natural gas are <u>diminishing</u>.

   (a) dwindling   **(b)** contracting   **(c)** swelling   **(d)** condensing

10. Many developing countries have debts that are too <u>huge</u> for them to handle.

    (a) miniscule   **(b)** minimal   **(c)** immense   **(d)** important

■■■ Chapter 11 ■■■

Idioms, Confusing Expressions, and Word Pairs

An *idiom* is an expression that you can't figure out from the individual words. There are thousands of idioms in English. The idioms in this section are some of the most common ones. Idioms are phrases like *by and large*. You may know what each of these words means separately, but the words taken in combination have an entirely different meaning.

In this section we will also look at some other easily confused words in English. Some of these are expressions using the verbs *make* or *do*, and others are word pairs that sound similar or have similar meanings.

SECTION I: IDIOMS

Conversation Practice

Read the following dialogue.

Bonnie: Are you going to the movies with us tonight, Ali?

Ali: No, I'm afraid that going to the movies is ***out of the question*** until I've finished my term paper.

Exercise 1

Work with a partner, with a group, or alone to answer the following questions.

1. From the conversation, do you think Ali will go to the movies?

   _____

2. What do you think *out of the question* means?

   _____

Conversation Practice

Read the following dialogue.

Bob: Do you think we'll see whooping cranes on our bird-watching trip?

Nina: I doubt it. Whooping cranes are an endangered species and sightings of them are *few and far between*.

Exercise 2

Work with a partner, with a group, or alone to answer the following questions.

1. From the conversation, do you think Bob and Nina will see a whooping crane?

   _____

2. What do you think *few and far between* means?

   _____

Conversation Practice

Read the following conversation.

Mai: Hi, Paul. I didn't think I'd *run into* you today.

Paul: My plans to go skiing this weekend *fell through*.

Mai: Then why don't you *drop by* my house for dinner tonight?

Paul: Thanks, that would be great.

Mai: Three of my girlfriends from school are coming, too.

Paul: Three girls! I'll feel like a *fish out of water!*

Mai: Oh, come on. It's time you *made* some new friends. Besides, you can help us *do* our homework afterward.

Paul: Aha! I knew there had to be *another* reason why you asked me to dinner.

Mai: I have to admit that besides the fact that you're my favorite cousin, we could really use your help.

Paul: All right then. But just remember that you owe me a favor.

Mai: I'll remember. Thanks, Paul. See you at six.

PRACTICE *Vocabulary*

Exercise 3

Work with a partner, with a group, or alone to answer the following questions.

1. Was Mai running when she met Paul?

   _____

2. From the conversation, what do you think *run into* means?

   _____

3. What happened to Paul's plans to go skiing?

   _____

4. Look at your answer above. What do the verb and preposition mean separately? Is this the meaning in the conversation? What do you think this idiom means?

   _____

   _____

5. What happens to a fish if you take it out of the water? What do you think *fish out of water* means?

   _____

6. What does Mai think it's time for Paul to do?

   _____

7. Give three expressions with the verb *make*.

   _____

   _____

8. What can Paul help Mai and her friends do?

   _____

9. Give three expressions with the verb *do*.

   _____

   _____

10. Is there a difference between *another* and *other*? What is the difference?

    _____

Strategies

- Listening to conversations and discussions in real life, on television, and in the movies will help you familiarize yourself with idiomatic expressions. It is important for you to develop an "ear" for the use of idioms and remember situations where you hear them used.

- There are different ways of remembering idioms. Some people memorize them. Other people remember them by associating a word in an idiom with a visual cue like an animal or an object.

- After you are able to remember the idiom, it is important to know in which situations and with whom you can use it. For example, replying "Search me" in answer to your teacher's question is not an appropriate way to answer someone in authority. Some idioms are only used between friends or peers.

- If you do not know or understand the idiom, look for clues in the context of the conversation.

   Example: "You look pale today. Are you feeling under the weather?"
   The word *pale* gives you a clue that the idiom *under the weather* means *ill* or *not well*.

   Example: **Girl:** I just broke my mother's favorite vase.
   Boy: Boy, are you in hot water!
   The girl's comment about breaking her mother's vase helps you understand that the idiom *in hot water* means *in trouble*.

Idioms (Group A)

above all = most important
as a matter of fact = in fact; to speak the truth
as a rule = generally; normally
be about to = be ready to; to be at the point of doing something
be an old hand at = be experienced
be fed up with = be out of patience with
be on one's own = live independently
be on the safe side = take no chances
be out of something = have no more in supply
be tired of = be bored with, frustrated with

Exercise 4

Using the list of idioms (Group A) on the previous page, complete the sentences and dialogues below. Change the verb form if necessary. Write the idiom on the blank line.

1. **Andrea:** Have you started studying for your biology test?

   Nicolai: Not yet, I was just _____.

2. Although it's warm today, I think you should take a sweater to_____

   _____.

3. Don't worry. I can change your tire. I'm an _____
   at it.

4. I have several goals in life, but _____, I
   want to be well-educated.

5. I wish I could offer you some fresh juice, but I'm _____

   _____ it.

6. **Alex:** I heard your brother got his own apartment.

   Rahel: That's right. He's finally going to live _____

   _____.

7. **Antonio:** What do you usually do on the weekends?

   Bill: _____ I stay at home, but next
   weekend I'm going to San Francisco.

8. I'll be happy when the new school year starts. I'm _____

   _____ vacation.

9. I'm _____ with this computer. It crashes all
   the time.

10. **Andres:** Are you going to the concert tonight?

    Brigitte: _____, I was just about to
    leave. Do you need a ride?

Idioms (Group B)

be up to one's ears = be extremely busy
be up to someone = be a person's responsibility or decision
be out of the question = be unacceptable, impossible
bite off more than one can chew = take on more than one can handle
break the ice = to be friendly with people one doesn't know
break the news = give bad news
brush up on = improve one's knowledge of something through study
bump into = meet unexpectedly
by and large = in general
by heart = by memory

Exercise 5

Circle the letter of the best answer to complete the sentence.

1. If Sean had to break the news to Mario about his damaged fender, Mario _____

   (a) already knew about it.

   (b) wouldn't be happy.

   (c) would be hearing about it for the first time.

2. If Hans bumped into Sara at the mall yesterday, he _____

   (a) didn't expect to see her.

   (b) had an appointment with her.

   (c) tried to knock her down.

3. If you're up to your ears with homework, you _____

   (a) don't have much to do.

   (b) have a lot to do.

   (c) can't wait to get started.

4. Peter started talking to Amanda about the weather, just to break the ice. Peter _____

   (a) spilled ice on Amanda.

   (b) acted in a cold manner.

   (c) tried to be friendly.

5. If you had to learn a list of dates by heart for your history exam, you _____

   (a) had to memorize them.

   (b) had to write them down.

   (c) had to feel good about them.

Copyright © 2002 Heinle & Heinle

144 ■■■   PRACTICE *Vocabulary*

6. Alfredo looked down the expert ski slope and realized he had bitten off more than he could chew. Alfredo _____

   (a) had chosen a ski area that was too difficult.

   (b) knew he could ski down the slope.

   (c) had his mouth full of food.

7. If Katherine brushed up on her French before her trip to France, she _____

   (a) made some plans.

   (b) did some cleaning.

   (c) did some studying.

8. If your teacher has told you it is out of the question for you to turn your term paper in late, you _____

   (a) must turn your paper in on time.

   (b) have some extra time.

   (c) don't have any more questions to ask your teacher.

9. If you know that by and large the weather is warm in Santo Domingo, you know that _____

   (a) it is extremely hot.

   (b) it is generally warm.

   (c) a big storm is coming.

10. If it's up to you to decide on a topic, the decision is _____

   (a) yours.

   (b) your teacher's.

   (c) in the syllabus.

Idioms (Group C)

by all means = absolutely, definitely
by no means = in no way
cheer up = be happy
come down with = become sick with
come up with = think of
count on = depend on
count one out = eliminate
die down = become quiet
do without = manage without something
drop by = visit informally; pay a short visit

Exercise 6

Write "C" on the blank line for the correct sentences and "I" for the incorrect sentences.

_____ 1. **Keisha:** Are you coming to my party tomorrow?

      Bob: Yes, you can count on me.

_____ 2. I'll be home all afternoon. Drop by any time.

_____ 3. I tried to think of an excuse, but I couldn't come down with one fast enough.

_____ 4. Mary was depressed, so I took her to a funny movie and she cheered up.

_____ 5. I forgot my notebook for class but I think I can do without it.

_____ 6. The wind was very strong at first but after a while it counted out.

_____ 7. **Thao:** You're looking a little bit tired today.

      Barb: Well, I think I'm coming up with the flu.

_____ 8. **Antonio:** May I share this bench with you?

      Malcolm: By no means. You're very welcome to sit here.

_____ 9. The cyclone passed over our farm and then the winds died down.

_____ 10. **Student:** Is it possible for me to take the exam again?

      Teacher: Take it again by all means. My goal is for you to learn the information.

Idioms (Group D)

every other = alternate
fall behind = fail to accomplish on time; not keep up
fall through = fail to happen or be completed
far cry from = completely different from
feel like = have a desire or wish for
feel up to = feel well enough to or capable of
few and far between = not often; rare
figure out = determine; reason out by thinking
fish out of water = out of one's element or natural environment
for good = permanently; forever

Exercise 7

Using the list of idioms (Group D) on the previous page, complete the sentences and dialogues below. Change the verb form if necessary. Write the idiom on the blank line.

1. I know you haven't been feeling well lately, but do you _____

   _____ a game today?

2. I don't have physics today. I have it _____
   day.

3. **Andres:** Are you going to be staying in the United States for a while?

   Kulwant: Yes, I'm here _____.

4. Michael felt like _____ because he was the
   only artist in a room full of bankers.

5. **Alex:** Let's stop and take a rest.

   Tahlia: No, we'd better keep walking or we'll _____
   the rest of the group.

6. Roberto, could you please help me? I can't _____
   how to answer this question.

7. Our plans to go diving _____ when I got
   sick.

8. **Peter:** What do you want to do today?

   Kerry: I _____ going to the beach.

9. This hotel is a _____ what they showed in
   the travel brochure.

10. At this time of year, tourists are _____.

Idioms (Group E)

for the time being = for now; temporarily
get rid of = give something away; sell, destroy, or throw away something
get the ball rolling = start something; make a beginning
get the hang of = understand; learn
give a hand = help
go without saying = to be understood; to be clear without needing to be stated
hang on = keep hold of; persevere
hard to come by = difficult to obtain
have a heart = have kind feelings; be understanding
have a hunch = have an idea based on feelings rather than reason

Exercise 8

Circle the letter of the best answer to complete the sentence.

1. After many hours with his tennis coach, Ron finally got the hang of serving. Ron
   _____

   (a) learned how to serve.

   (b) hung up his tennis racquet.

   (c) still doesn't know how to serve.

2. If the special edition of the book is hard to come by, it _____

   (a) can be found in any bookstore.

   (b) is a hardcover edition.

   (c) is difficult to find.

3. If Jan finally got rid of his old football, he _____

   (a) is saving it for the future.

   (b) no longer has it.

   (c) loaned it to a friend for a short time.

4. If you have a hunch that Sandy will be at the party tonight, you _____

   (a) don't think she'll be there.

   (b) think she'll be there.

   (c) wonder if she'll be there.

5. If Mai Lin was the one who got the ball rolling on your group science project,
   she _____

   (a) put off working on the project.

   (b) rolled a ball around as part of the project.

   (c) got the group started on the project.

6. If you gave your neighbor a hand with her groceries, you _____

   (a) helped her.

   (b) avoided her.

   (c) shook hands with her.

7. Sidney used a bit of wire to fix the cage for the time being. Sidney _____

   (a) permanently fixed the cage.

   (b) temporarily fixed the cage.

   (c) didn't know how to fix the cage.

8. If Rebecca is hanging on to an old clock, she _____

   (a) is keeping it.

   (b) is holding it in her hands.

   (c) is going to throw it away.

9. If it goes without saying that cheating is punished by expulsion, you _____

   (a) know it without being told.

   (b) have to be told.

   (c) you say it all the time.

10. If the bus driver had a heart and stopped right in front of our house, he _____

   (a) was kind.

   (b) had a heart transplant.

   (c) had a heart attack.

Idioms (Group F)

hop to it = get started on something right away
hit it off = get along well with someone
ill at ease = uncomfortable
in hot water = in trouble
in the dark = not informed
in the long run = looking toward the future; eventually
ins and outs = all the details; the various parts and difficulties
iron out = remove the difficulties or find a solution
jump to conclusions = arrive too quickly at a decision or opinion
keep one's eye on = watch closely

Exercise 9

Write "C" on the blank line for the correct sentences and "I" for the incorrect sentences.

_____ 1. You may not like getting a flu shot now but in the dark it will be good for you.

_____ 2. Please keep your eye on the children while I go to the store.

_____ 3. Until her friends arrived, she felt in hot water because she didn't know anyone in the room.

_____ 4. The minute he looked at the test he knew he was jumping to conclusions because he hadn't studied.

_____ 5. You'd better hit it off, or you'll never be ready in time.

_____ 6. Ahmed is an excellent tour guide because he knows all the ins and outs of traveling.

_____ 7. Don't worry about your misunderstanding with the principal. I'll get it ironed out for you.

_____ 8. The stock market is a good investment in the long run.

_____ 9. We told her she had to hop to it if she expected to be ready in time.

_____ 10. We felt extremely ill at ease because we were dressed too casually for the event.

Idioms (Group G)

keep one's fingers crossed = hope that nothing goes wrong
keep on one's toes = be ready for action; prepared
learn the ropes = learn the rules and routines of a place or activity
make ends meet = to have just enough money for one's needs
mean to = intentionally or on purpose
might as well = to have no strong reason not to
next to nothing = almost nothing; very inexpensive
not to mention = in addition
off balance = unaware; off guard
on the go = busy

Exercise 10

Circle the letter of the best answer to complete the sentence.

1. We are keeping our fingers crossed that the weather will be nice for graduation day. We _____
   (a) are wishing for nice weather.
   (b) have been told the weather will be fine.
   (c) don't really care about the weather.

2. If Leslie caught you off balance, she _____
   (a) surprised you.
   (b) stopped you from falling.
   (c) played catch with you.

3. Jessie paid next to nothing for her new backpack. She _____
   (a) paid a lot for it.
   (b) got a bargain.
   (c) got it for free.

4. If Beth has learned the ropes on her new job, she _____
   (a) has a lot to learn.
   (b) has a job using ropes.
   (c) knows her job.

5. Jamal decided to take an extra language course just to stay on his toes. Jamal _____
   (a) wants to be prepared.
   (b) likes to exercise.
   (c) knows his job.

PRACTICE *Vocabulary*

6. If Juan earns just enough money to make ends meet, he _____

   (a) earns more than he needs.

   (b) doesn't earn enough to live on.

   (c) earns just enough to pay his bills.

7. If the pitcher didn't mean to hit the batter, he _____

   (a) did it on purpose.

   (b) wasn't a good sport.

   (c) didn't intend to do it.

8. If you're constantly on the go, you _____

   (a) aren't very busy.

   (b) are doing something all the time.

   (c) have some bad habits.

9. If I have to take care of both my sisters, not to mention my nephews, I have to take care of my nephews _____

   (a) in addition to my sisters.

   (b) and teach my nephews addition.

   (c) instead of my sisters.

10. You might as well take the exam, since you have nothing to lose. You _____

   (a) should take it.

   (b) will do well on it.

   (c) shouldn't take it.

Idioms (Group H)

on pins and needles = nervous; anxious
on purpose = deliberately; intentionally
on the blink = not working properly
on the right track = thinking or doing something correctly
on the tip of one's tongue = to be about to remember something
once in a blue moon = rarely; almost never
pick up the tab = pay the cost of something
piece of cake = easy
play it by ear = act spontaneously; without planning
pull it off = accomplish

Exercise 11

Using the list of idioms (Group H) on the previous page, complete the sentences and dialogues below. Change the verb form if necessary. Write the idiom on the blank line.

1. Since Maurice does not like the ballet, we only go

   _____.

2. **Andrea:** Why didn't your mom drive you to school today?

   Emily: She couldn't drive. Our car is _____ again.

3. **Meera:** Do you remember who starred in that movie?

   Max: I know who it is, but I can't remember her name. It's right

   _____.

4. **Antonio:** Let me help you pay for lunch.

   Jo: No. Since it's your birthday, I'll

   _____.

5. **Andy:** How was the test? Was it easy?

   Naomi: No problem. It was a _____.

6. **Anna:** Do you have plans for the holiday weekend?

   Juan: No. I'm going to _____.

7. I may not have my problem solved, but at least I know I'm

   _____.

8. I have all the tools for this job, but I'm still not sure I can

   _____.

9. I'm sorry I spilled soup all over you. Believe me, I didn't do it

   _____.

10. We'll be _____ until we hear who won the poetry contest.

PRACTICE *Vocabulary*

Idioms (Group 1)

> **pull one's leg** = fool someone
> **quite a few** = several
> **right away** = immediately
> **run for office** = compete for an elected position
> **save one's breath** = to keep silent because talking would not achieve anything
> **you can say that again** = I agree completely
> **a stone's throw** = short distance
> **search me** = I don't know
> **serve one right** = to be deserving of (usually something bad)
> **sleep on it** = think about something for a while

Exercise 12

Write "C" on the blank line for the correct sentences and "I" for the incorrect sentences.

_____ 1. **Kim:** I failed my math test.
Antonne: Well, it pulls your leg for not studying.

_____ 2. **Stephen:** Have you ever been to Yosemite National Park?
Stan: Yes, I've gone there quite a few times.

_____ 3. When she told me she'd won $25,000, I thought she was saving her breath.

_____ 4. We'll have to get to the library right away, as it will be closing soon.

_____ 5. **Kei:** Do you live very far from here?
Dandan: No. It's just quite a few away.

_____ 6. Class elections are coming up and I've decided to search me.

_____ 7. **Anna:** I can't decide which calculator I want to buy.
Juan: Then why don't you sleep on it and choose one tomorrow?

_____ 8. **Sean:** The weather is absolutely perfect today.
Emily: You can say that again!

_____ 9. **Bic:** You won the lottery!
Andres: I know you're just pulling my leg.

_____ 10. **Maria:** Do you know the population of Tegucigalpa?
Jorge: Search me.

Idioms (Group J)

straighten up = make tidy	
take a break = rest for a while	
think nothing of it = that's all right	
throw cold water on = discourage; lessen enthusiasm for	
to say the least = to understate	
under the weather = ill; not well	
well worth the trouble = deserving the inconvenience	
whole new ballgame = an entirely different situation	
with flying colors = very well	
without a hitch = without difficulty or delay	

Exercise 13

Complete the sentence or dialogue with idioms from the above list. Change the verb form if necessary. Write the idiom on the blank lines.

1. I'm sorry I won't be able to go to the art exhibit with you tonight, but I'm feeling

    _____.

2. **Tomas:** Did your presentation go well yesterday?
    Sennet: Yes, there were no problems. Everything went off _____

    _____.

3. I am so excited about going to the desert this weekend. I hope you are not going

    to _____ my plans by saying you won't go.

4. I was so happy when I received my grades yesterday. I passed all of my courses

    _____.

5. We're getting tired. Let's _____.

6. **An:** Boy, is your room a mess!
    Emily: I know. Mom told me I can't leave until I _____ it

    _____.

7. **Mother:** Did you have a hard time finding your grandmother a birthday
    present?
    Daughter: Yes, but when I saw her expression when she opened it, I knew it was

    _____.

8. **Maria:** Thank you so much for helping me get my car started.

   José: _____. It was no trouble at all.

9. Now that the government has changed, it's a _____

   _____.

10. _____, Latin American politics are volatile.

SECTION II:
CONFUSING EXPRESSIONS AND WORD PAIRS

There are a number of words in English that often cause problems because they have similar meanings or sound alike. One of the most common errors involves the use of the verbs *make* and *do*.

Strategies

- Just like with idioms, listening will help you get an "ear" for expressions with *make* and *do*. You may be able to "hear" that one verb sounds better than the other with an expression.

- You can learn the expressions with *make* or *do* by using the same methods as for idioms, memorizing them or using visual reminders or other methods that work for you.

- The following exercises will help you familiarize yourself with some common *make* and *do* expressions. Make a list of expressions with these verbs. Every time you hear or see a new expression with one of these verbs, add it to your list.

- The structures in which some confusing words are used will help you recognize and use them correctly.

Expressions with *make* and *do*

Many languages have only one verb for **do** and **make**. In English, the verb *to do* means *to perform* or *to act*, while the verb *make* means *to produce* or *to create*. These two verbs are found in a number of fixed expressions. If you don't understand some of these expressions, look them up in your dictionary or ask a native English speaker to explain them to you.

Expressions with *make*

make a mistake	make a plan
make war	make an investment
make a comparison	make an offer
make a discovery	make a choice
make use of	make an attempt
make a profit	make a decision
make a suggestion	make a forecast
make enemies	make a complaint
make a contribution	make a plan
make an escape	make a confession
make a fortune	make money
make amends	make way
make friends	make progress
make trouble	make sure
make room	make an improvement
make a difference	make a distinction
make a journey	make a prediction

Expressions with *do*

do one's duty	do harm
do homework	do research
do justice to	do an assignment
do business with	do one's best
do work	do a service
do wrong	do damage
do good	do a favor
do without	do a kindness
do nothing	do a job

PRACTICE *Vocabulary*

Exercise 14

Some of these words can be used with *make* and some with *do*. Circle the letter of the verb that best completes the expression, then write the correct word on the blank line.

1. _____ a journey **(a)** do **(b)** make

2. _____ a favor **(a)** do **(b)** make

3. _____ a service **(a)** do **(b)** make

4. _____ a fortune **(a)** do **(b)** make

5. _____ good **(a)** do **(b)** make

6. _____ money **(a)** do **(b)** make

7. _____ a choice **(a)** do **(b)** make

8. _____ trouble **(a)** do **(b)** make

9. _____ sure **(a)** do **(b)** make

10. _____ enemies **(a)** do **(b)** make

11. _____ a complaint **(a)** do **(b)** make

12. _____ nothing **(a)** do **(b)** make

13. _____ friends **(a)** do **(b)** make

14. _____ progress **(a)** do **(b)** make

15. _____ use of something **(a)** do **(b)** make

16. _____ an investment **(a)** do **(b)** make

17. _____ wrong **(a)** do **(b)** make

Exercise 15

List the following words under the correct heading, either *She made* or *She did*.

her best	a difference	plans
her duty	a distinction	room
research	a contribution	an improvement
amends	without	her job
a confession	her homework	a prediction
an escape		

She made

_____   _____

_____   _____

_____   _____

_____   _____

_____   _____

She did

_____   _____

_____   _____

_____   _____

_____   _____

PRACTICE *Vocabulary*

Exercise 16

Circle the correct word to complete each sentence.

1. Albert Einstein's theories (made / done) a great contribution to the development of modern science.

2. Bats can hear and distinguish insects by the number of wing beats per second the insect (makes / does).

3. (Doing / Making) cloth with synthetic fibers requires less labor than with natural fibers.

4. Nostradamus (made / did) predictions for the year 1999 in the sixteenth century.

5. All possible colors can be (made / done) by mixing three primary colors together in different proportions.

6. Eli Whitney's invention (did / made) much to improve the American cotton industry.

7. *Pioneer* and *Voyager* are the names of two kinds of American space probes that have (made / done) important discoveries about the solar system.

8. Richard Hoe's invention of the steam cylinder rotary press in 1847 (did / made) it possible for newspapers to be printed at a faster rate.

9. Many advances have been (made / done) in the field of communication through the use of fiber optics.

10. Elizabeth Blackwell (made / did) it possible for women to enter professions that had previously excluded them.

Confusing Word Pairs (Group A)

like and *alike*

Another pair of words that often causes problems is *like* and *alike*. They have very similar meanings, but are used in different patterns.

Like X, Y, . . .
> Like my sister, I decided to study German.

X, like Y, . . .
> Katie, like Rebecca, wants to study Italian.

X is like Y . . .
> John is like Jill because they both love to travel.

but

X and Y are alike . . .
> Sidney and Seymour are alike because they both prefer fish to beef.

---

unlike and *not alike*

In the negative form, **unlike** and **not alike** have very similar meanings, too, but are used in different patterns.

Unlike X, Y . . .
> Unlike Veronica, José has already turned in all his applications.

X, unlike Y . . .
> Salt, unlike sugar, is tasted on the sides of the tongue.

X is unlike Y . . .
> Democracy is unlike a dictatorship because there are free elections in a democracy.

but

X and Y are not alike . . .
> I don't know why Kathy and Cristina are always compared since they are not alike in any way.

PRACTICE *Vocabulary*

Exercise 17

Circle the correct word to complete each sentence.

1. (Alike / Like) butterflies, moths can be dull-colored or brightly hued.

2. (Alike / Like) other beans, lima beans are seeds that grow in pods.

3. (Not alike / Unlike) oxygen, which is changed in our bodies into carbon dioxide, nitrogen goes back into the air.

4. (Like / Alike) Yellowstone National Park in Wyoming, Tongariro National Park in New Zealand is famous for its hot-springs system.

5. The first English settlers, (alike / like) the Native Americans, planted corn and ate pumpkin and squash.

6. Keratin is found in feathers and in our fingernails (alike / like).

7. (Like / Alike) animals, plants need vitamins for growth and development.

8. (Unlike / Not alike) animals, which are mobile, plants are largely stationary.

9. Neanderthal man was not greatly (alike / unlike) modern man in physical structure.

10. Settlers, (alike / unlike) tourists, stay permanently in a new country.

Confusing Word Pairs (Group B)
affect (v.) and *effect* (n.)

Affect means to influence; *effect* means result.
    The tranquilizer was not affecting the animal.
    The tranquilizer had no effect on the animal.

after (prep.) and *afterward* (adv.)

After means following in time, or later than; *afterward* means at a later time.
    I will see you after the test.
    I will see you afterward.

almost (adv.) and *most* (adj.)

Almost means very nearly; *most* means the greatest part.
    Almost everyone passed the test.
    Most students received a passing grade.

among (prep.) and between (prep.)

Among is used for three or more persons or things; *between* is used for two persons or things.

> The work was distributed between Paul and John.
> The work was distributed among members of the team.

amount (n.) and number (n.)

Amount is used with noncount nouns; *number* is used with count nouns.

> A great amount of money was spent on housing.
> A great number of houses were being built.

another (adj.) and other (adj.)

Another means one more and is used before a singular noun or alone. *Other* means the remaining of two or more. It is used before a plural noun or before a singular noun when preceded by a determiner.

> She needs another piece of paper.
> I prefer the other color for this room.
> We have other ideas about this project.

because (adv.) and because of (prep.)

Because introduces an adverb clause and is followed by a subject and verb; *because of* is followed by a noun clause.

> Because it was dark, we could not see.
> Because of the darkness, we could not see.

before (adv.) and ago (adv.)

Before means at an earlier time; *ago* means in the past.

> She graduated three years before we did (eight years ago).
> We graduated five years ago.

Confusing Word Pairs (Group C)
differ (v.) and different (adj.)

Differ and *different* mean not the same. They are both followed by *from*.

> These two words differ from each other as parts of speech.
> These two words are not different from each other in meaning.

Copyright © 2002 Heinle & Heinle

PRACTICE *Vocabulary*

fewer (adj.) and less (adj.)

Both words mean a small quantity or amount. *Fewer* is used with count nouns and *less* is used with noncount nouns.

There were fewer birds this year.

There was less noise.

hard (adj.) and hardly (adv.)

Hard means difficult; *hardly* means scarcely or barely.

The reading passages were hard.

He spoke so fast she could hardly understand.

lonely (adj.) and alone (adj.)

Lonely means feeling unhappy and abandoned; *alone* means without others.

He had no friends and felt lonely.

He likes to hike in the mountains alone.

near (adj.) and nearly (adv.)

Near means not far; *nearly* means almost.

The city is near the ocean.

We nearly missed the bus.

old (adj.) and age (n.)

Old means advanced in age; *age* means the period of time a person or thing has existed.

Despite being old, my grandparents are fit and healthy.

Mozart composed music at a very young age.

percent (adv.) and percentage (n.)

Percent means one part in each 100; *percentage* means the proportion as a whole of 100.

The five oceans of the world cover 71 percent of the world's surface.

The percentage of people dying from this disease is increasing every year.

tall (adj.) and high (adj.)

Tall means something or someone that measures more than average height; *high* means that the top of something is a long distance from the ground. *Tall* is used for people and also for things that are both narrow and high.

There is a high wall around the palace.

George Washington was a tall man.

Sequoias are tall trees.

End of Chapter Test

I.

Read the following dialogues and answer the questions. Circle the letter of the best answer.

1. **Boy:** I heard you have a part in the school play tonight.
   Girl: Yes, and I'm on pins and needles.

   How does the girl feel?

   (a) happy   **(b)** angry   **(c)** nervous   **(d)** confused

2. **Woman:** Do you get pay raises where you work?
   Man: Yes, but they are few and far between.

   What does the man mean?

   (a) He gets lots of raises at his job.

   (b) There are no raises given where he works.

   (c) They don't give raises very often where he works.

   (d) He has to go far to get a raise.

3. **Woman:** Have you made our plane reservations yet?
   Man: No, I'm leaving it up to you.

   What does the man mean?

   (a) Leave him alone.

   (b) The woman should make the plane reservations.

   (c) Let him make the reservations.

   (d) Get someone else to make the reservations.

4. **Man:** I don't want that puppy in the house.
   Woman: Oh, have a heart.

   What does the woman mean?

   (a) She agrees with the man.

   (b) She wants the man to hold his heart.

   (c) She wants the man to feel sympathy for the puppy.

   (d) She wants the man to kiss the puppy.

5. **Man:** How was your blind date last night?
   Woman: We hit it off right away.

   What does the woman mean?

   (a) She had a quarrel with her date.

   (b) She and her date left quickly.

   (c) She and her date knocked something down.

   (d) She and her date got along well.

6. **Woman:** I should tell them they need more decorations.
   Man: They never listen to anyone, so save your breath.

   What does the man mean?

   (a) Don't say anything.   **(c)** Make some suggestions.

   (b) Hold your breath.   **(d)** Listen to the others.

7. **Man:** I think something must be wrong because Yves wasn't home when I called.
   Woman: Oh, you are always jumping to conclusions.

   What does the woman mean?

   (a) He is thoughtful about things.

   (b) He arrives at opinions too quickly.

   (c) He can't sit still.

   (d) He doesn't know how to make a decision.

8. **Woman:** Is this computer program similar to the one you've been using?
   Man: No, it's a whole new ballgame.

   What does the man mean?

   (a) The programs are alike.

   (b) The programs are computer games.

   (c) The programs are very different.

   (d) The programs are easy.

9. **Woman:** Aren't you fed up with your noisy brothers?
   Man: They don't bother me anymore. I'm wearing earplugs.

   What does the woman's question mean?

   (a) Does he like his brothers?

   (b) Have his brothers already eaten?

   (c) Is he losing patience with his brothers?

   (d) Does he have any problems with brothers?

10. **Woman:** I have a great idea for the graduation dinner.

    Man: I knew you'd come up with something.

    What does the man mean?

    (a) He knew she would bring him something.

    (b) He wasn't expecting her to have a plan.

    (c) He thought she would be coming to see him.

    (d) He was sure she would think up an idea.

II.

The following sentences contain some of the confusing words you have learned. Some sentences are correct and some are not. Write "C" on the blank line for correct sentences and "I" for incorrect sentences.

_____ 1. Chickens start to lay eggs at eighteen weeks age.

_____ 2. Nearly eight percent of the Earth's crust is made of aluminum.

_____ 3. When the original thirteen states formed a Union, afterward the American Revolution, each representative wanted to have the capital in his own state.

_____ 4. Our Milky Way, alike other similar galaxies, contains stars of varying sizes.

_____ 5. Sequoia trees, some of which are more than 3000 years ago, are among the tallest and oldest trees in the world.

_____ 6. Not alike humans, gorillas live in largely permanent family groups.

_____ 7. The Galapagos tortoise lives on the Galapagos Islands near the equator.

_____ 8. Fog is the affect of the cooling of warm, moist air.

_____ 9. Many people make the mistake of thinking that pandas are bears, when they are actually related to the American raccoon.

PRACTICE *Vocabulary*